Cambridge Elements ≡

Elements in the Economics of Emerging Markets
edited by
Bruno S. Sergi
Harvard University

TOWARDS A THEORY OF "SMART" SOCIAL INFRASTRUCTURES AT THE BASE OF THE PYRAMID

A Study of India

Sandeep Goyal
L. M. Thapar School of Management

Bruno S. Sergi
Harvard University

CAMBRIDGE
UNIVERSITY PRESS

CAMBRIDGE
UNIVERSITY PRESS

University Printing House, Cambridge CB2 8BS, United Kingdom

One Liberty Plaza, 20th Floor, New York, NY 10006, USA

477 Williamstown Road, Port Melbourne, VIC 3207, Australia

314–321, 3rd Floor, Plot 3, Splendor Forum, Jasola District Centre,
New Delhi – 110025, India

79 Anson Road, #06–04/06, Singapore 079906

Cambridge University Press is part of the University of Cambridge.

It furthers the University's mission by disseminating knowledge in the pursuit of
education, learning, and research at the highest international levels of excellence.

www.cambridge.org
Information on this title: www.cambridge.org/9781108794800
DOI: 10.1017/9781108882170

First published 2020

A catalogue record for this publication is available from the British Library.

ISBN 978-1-108-79480-0 Paperback
ISSN 2631-8598 (online)
ISSN 2631-858X (print)

Cambridge University Press has no responsibility for the persistence or accuracy of
URLs for external or third-party internet websites referred to in this publication
and does not guarantee that any content on such websites is, or will remain,
accurate or appropriate.

Towards a Theory of "Smart" Social Infrastructures at the Base of the Pyramid

A Study of India

Elements in the Economics of Emerging Markets

DOI: 10.1017/9781108882170
First published online: May 2020

Sandeep Goyal
L. M. Thapar School of Management

Bruno S. Sergi
Harvard University

Author for correspondence: Bruno S. Sergi, bsergi@fas.harvard.edu

Abstract: The primary focus of this Element is to understand the rise of "smart" social infrastructures in Base of the Pyramid emerging markets like India. It has been observed that new focus areas and frontiers of global economy are taking shape where social and environmental outcomes, along with economic performance, are considered to be the collective parameters for success or failure of the businesses. This has led to the emergence of new models of entrepreneurship, namely, for-profit social businesses. These new models are adopted by problem-solving social innovators who are driven by the social and environmental mission, besides economic gains. Sustainability and overall success of social businesses rely on smart social infrastructure comprising availability of an incubation ecosystem for social start-ups, access to long-term capital, availability of a digital ecosystem, adoption of circular business models, and focus on collaborations, partnerships, and networking with diverse stakeholders.

Keywords: base of the pyramid, BoP, social business models, smart infrastructure, digital ecosystem, circular economy

ISBNs: 9781108794800 (PB), 9781108882170 (OC)
ISSNs: 2631-8598 (online), 2631-858X (print)

Contents

1 Introduction

During the beginning of the twenty-first century, Prahalad and Hart pushed the radical idea that global businesses should look upon the underserved poor as customers who could be engaged profitably with the right product, service offerings, and business models, rather than left aside as beneficiaries. They made a broad argument that approximately 4 billion people around the world were living in poverty, relying on informal market setups or government subsidies and grants for the fulfillment of their basic needs, and representing a vibrant underserved consumer market waiting for formal market inclusion with the right combination of value and price-based solutions (Prahalad & Hart, 2002). This idea of merging profit and purpose for the low-income segment was coined by Prahalad and Hart as Bottom of the Pyramid, also known as Base of the Pyramid (BoP) (Prahalad & Hart, 2002). During the last two decades (2000–2020), BoP as a radical concept has created a lot of buzz among academicians, businesses, governments, development institutions, etc., which in turn has generated a lot of positive and negative conversations around the feasibility and fitment of for-profit businesses in the BoP market. The central theme revolves around ways and means of alleviating poverty with or without the involvement of for-profit businesses.

During 2000–2020, the global poverty landscape has undergone a significant transformation in terms of socioeconomic inclusion and growth prospects, technology advancement and penetration, rise of social businesses, and growing awareness regarding environmental hazards. Following are the key highlights, which demand a fresh look at the BoP segment.

First, there has been a significant reduction in the count of people living in extreme poverty. According to World Bank estimates, around 1.1. billion people have moved out of extreme poverty (<$1.9 per person per day at 2002 PPP)[1] between 1990–2015 (World Bank, 2019). Nearly 1.85 billion people lived on an average daily income of $1.9 per day in 1990. This figure came down to around 736 million people in 2015 (World Bank, 2019). As a result, overall count of

---

[1] PPP (Purchasing Power Parity) relates to the rate of currency conversion that equalizes the purchasing power of different currencies by adjusting the price level differences between countries. PPPs are also known as price relatives that reflect the ratio of prices in national currencies of the same good or service in different countries. According to World Bank estimates, INR 18.15 is equivalent to USD 1 in terms of PPP in 2018. PPP calculation leads to the inter-country comparison in the real terms of GDP and its component expenditures. GDP represents the economic size of the countries and the economic well-being of their residents on a per-capita basis. Doing PPP analysis is the first step towards converting the GDP and its major aggregates, expressed in national currencies, into a common currency. www.oecd.org/std/prices-ppp/purcha singpowerparities-frequentlyaskedquestionsfaqs.htm; https://data.worldbank.org/indicator/PA .NUS.PPP?locations=IN (last accessed on 29 June 2019).

people in the BoP segment has declined from around 4 billion in 2002 to 3.4 billion in 2017 (Prahalad, 2019; CS Global Wealth Report, 2017).[2]

Second, there has been consistent growth in the number of people on this planet. Globally, the population has increased from around 6.1 billion in 2000 to 7.5 billion in 2019 (UNDESA, 2019). This implies an ongoing need for concentrated action towards setting up a formal market ecosystem for the BoP segment, as well as environmental sustainability.

Third, internet and mobile penetration among the masses and economy pricing has eased out the last-mile challenges for social businesses in terms of creating last-mile market awareness, connection and reach, as well as offering services like bank payment, information, timely communication, etc. (Prahalad, 2019).

Fourth, the overall poverty challenge still remains a stiff target despite the progress made over the last two decades. Growth in population is mainly happening in African and South Asian economies. Also, the majority of the global poor, especially the extreme poor, is becoming concentrated in these developing and underdeveloped economies. If this population growth and socioeconomic inequality trend continues, then soon more than nine out ten extreme poor individuals will be concentrated in sub-Saharan Africa and South Asian economies (Prahalad, 2019; World Bank, 2019).

Fifth, there has been a significant shift in the wealth concentration at the top versus bottom of the income pyramid. In 2000, 20 percent of the population controlled around 85 percent of global income (Prahalad, 2019). According to CS Global Wealth Report (2019), the richest 10 percent of people own 82 percent of global wealth with the top 1 percent controlling more than 45 percent of global wealth.

Due to these factors, it becomes necessary to realign today's BoP conversation from alleviating poverty to reducing the growing socioeconomic disparity and deep inequality. How and which types of smart social infrastructure can reduce the growing inequality between rich and poor? How can BoP individuals gain access to better income opportunities and the formal market ecosystem for the fulfillment of their basic needs?

The next question that comes up is: what exactly is the socioeconomic status of BoP individuals or households? The BoP segment comprises low-income people, the majority of whom are primarily illiterate or semi-literate and lack access to the formal market ecosystem for the fulfillment of their basic needs

---

[2] BoP segment of 4 billion comprises individuals earning less than $3,000 per year (at US 2002 PPP level) (Hammond et al., 2007; Prahalad and Hart, 2002).

like food, energy, water, healthcare, education, cash flow, insurance, and housing. Due to insufficient income levels, lack of focus and attention by formal business enterprises, and scarcity of basic infrastructure in urban slums and rural areas, BoP individuals face significant challenges in making a transition from an informal economy to a formal market ecosystem to address their day-to-day needs (Neuwirth, 2012). Multiple approaches have been tried by governments (via subsidies and grants), enterprises (via Corporate Social Responsibility (CSR) initiatives), and global institutions to pay attention to the basic needs of the BoP segment and design an affordable, accessible, and acceptable ecosystem for the productive engagement of poor individuals in the formal market economy.

Another question that comes up is: what kind of inequality and challenges exist at the BoP. More than 1.1 billion people lack access to electricity and an estimated 2.8 billion people rely on biomass, coal, and kerosene oil for cooking and lighting in 2016 (IEA, 2017). Around 790 million people lack access to clean drinking water and an estimated 2.5 billion people do not have adequate sanitation facilities (CDCP, 2016). Similarly, access to healthcare remains a challenge especially in the developing economies across Africa and South Asia. Around 0.3 million (810 women daily) die every year during pregnancy or childbirth (WHO-IMR, 2019). More than 4.1 million infants die within the first year of life (WHO-MMR, 2019). Despite a comprehensive healthcare ecosystem across nations, there is a missing link resulting in so many maternal and infant deaths every year. Millions of people globally fall below the poverty line every year due to uneventful health issues in their families resulting in spiralling healthcare expenditure. This effects, for example, around 55 million Indians annually (Nagarajan, 2018). These people lack access to health insurance and rely on day-to-day earnings for addressing their basic needs. Regarding financial inclusion, there are more than 2 billion people and around 200 million MSMEs (Medium, Small, and Micro Enterprises) lacking access to the formal market setup for savings and short-term credit facilities (McKinsey Global Institute, 2016). Due to lack of financial inclusion, BoP people and businesses face poverty penalties and rely on the informal market setup for short-term money needs at substantial interest levels. This vicious cycle of private loans and high interest rates pushes BoP people and their future generations further below the poverty line.

Gradually, for-profit enterprises are realizing the socioeconomic potential, positive branding, and business logic behind targeting the unmet needs of the BoP segment. This has resulted in growth of social businesses, as well as transformation in CSR strategy of commercial enterprises from "pay-back business model looking at BoP as beneficiaries" to "self-sustainable business model looking at BoP as customers." Then there are government institutions, nongovernmental organizations (NGOs), and community based organizations (CBOs) that are also moving beyond a philanthropic setup to self-sustainable business models at the BoP.

Social businesses are driven by a new belief that BoP individuals can no longer be considered as beneficiaries willing to accept anything but need to be looked upon as a high-potential consumer segment looking for right-value offerings in accordance with their willingness to pay (WTP) and ability to pay (ATP). Social businesses are finding innovative solutions to expand the last-mile connectivity and reach at the BoP by leveraging digital technologies for last-mile awareness building, accessibility, and availability, as well as engaging the locals across the value chain for affordability and social acceptance. All these social businesses are looking at the diverse needs of the BoP segment, ranging from basic requirements like food, energy, healthcare, water, sanitation, housing, education, financing, and insurance to other important needs like communication, market-based setups, higher-income opportunities, information, etc. In fact, more and more social businesses are looking at the BoP segment not only as a potential consumer base but also in terms of suppliers, employees, producers, micro-entrepreneurs, and change agents (UNDP & Deloitte, 2016).

The rapid advancement and growth of information and communication technologies (ICT) has emerged as one of the key levers in the success of social business models at the BoP. Over the years, rapid growth and penetration of digital technologies has led to the emergence of scalable, innovative, and low-cost social business models targeting the basic needs of the BoP segment. Last-mile connectivity, channels for sales and distribution, and building customer relationships are among the major challenges for enterprises targeting the BoP segment (SSG Advisors, 2016). Digital technologies have played a significant role as a key resource in addressing these last-mile challenges in a cost-effective manner. ICT has emerged as a significant enabler in bringing about the economic, social, and political transformation at the BoP. Affordable pricing and increasing quality of ICT related services has led to significant penetration among the BoP segment. This in turn has created an effective channel for the government and enterprises to build awareness, bridge accessibility barriers, and provide affordable solutions and value offerings at the BoP (Spence et al., 2010). ICT has enabled the last-mile reach of market-based offerings like banking and financial transactions, marketing and distribution, online employment opportunities, telemedicine, online education, access to global market for the rural suppliers, access to information like weather forecasts and market rates for different crops, etc. Besides economic well-being, ICT penetration is acting as a significant enabler for public services like disbursement of pensions and subsidies, as well as participation in different government schemes. ICT is increasingly being seen as a catalyst and enabler for economic growth and social advancement globally. Adoption of ICT leads to operational efficiency, better transparency, social inclusion, and newer business models having wider connectivity and reach among the masses (EIU, 2007). High-speed internet and communication technologies are transforming the delivery of public services to the last-mile people living in rural areas, as well as providing access to the formal market ecosystem for micro and small entrepreneurs at the BoP. For example, increasing numbers of rural artisans and craftsmen from India are selling their goods globally via e-commerce platforms. This amplifies the socioeconomic impact of digital platforms on the lives of poor people living in rural and semi-urban areas and having no formal market experience. The farmers of South Africa are selling their produce directly to far-away restaurants and hotels via mobile phones thereby increasing their income levels, as well as avoiding exploitation by intermediaries. The rapid expansion and scale of Safaricom's M-PESA in Kenya proves the disruptive role of digital technologies in creating transformative social and economic impact among the poor in developing economies.

The primary focus of this Element is to understand the rise of "smart" social infrastructures in BoP emerging markets like India. Addressing this objective required looking at the BoP context in terms of existing challenges, alternatives, and the effectiveness of solutions across the need segments. This Element is divided into the following sections. Section 2 focuses on understanding the BoP as a market context. This includes understanding the key definitions and research focus areas related to BoP as well as identifying the key challenges and institutional voids faced by the BoP segment. This is followed by a review of the existing research literature on BoP. Section 3 highlights the preparatory phase including details about research methodology, sampling approach, and data collection. Section 4 analyzes the context, operation, and business models of social businesses that have been identified for this study. Section 5 connects the dots and summarizes the key focus areas that need attention for success at the BoP. Section 6 highlights limitations and future recommendations. Finally, Section 7 concludes the study by summarizing key points of smart social infrastructures at the BoP that can lead to a win-win relationship as well as significant socioeconomic impact at the BoP.

2 Understanding BoP: Market Context and Research Literature

2.1 BoP Market Context: Potential and Significance

Globally, the population has grown significantly over the years from 2.6 billion in 1950 to 7.4 billion in 2019 (UN-POP, 2019). Going by the current growth trends and increasing longevity, global population count is expected to reach

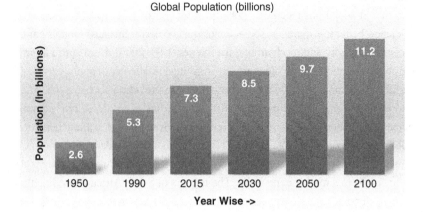

Figure 1 Global population trends (in billions)
Source: UN-POP (2019)

9.7 billion by 2050 (Figure 1). A few interesting points come up from the global population distribution and growth trends.

First, in 2019, around 61 percent of the global population lives in Asia (4.7 billion), 17 percent in Africa (1.3 billion), 10 percent in Europe (750 million), 5 percent in North America (370 million), and the remaining 7 percent in Latin America. At the country level, China is the most populated with more than 1.44 billion people followed by India with a population of more than 1.39 billion (UN-POP, 2019).

Second, Africa will account for more than 50 percent of the population growth between 2019 and 2050. The population of sub-Saharan Africa is expected to double by 2050. This signifies that future growth of businesses will be driven by developing and underdeveloped economies as these countries will account for the majority of the global population, reaching around 95 percent by 2050.

This population demographics and growth pattern has huge implications for global businesses and institutions. While the majority of the population in developed economies is categorized as of the mid- or upper-income segment and as having access to formal market ecosystems for the fulfillment of their basic needs, the same is not the case with developing economies where the majority of the population lies in the BoP category (Esposito et al., 2012). For example, India is one of the high-growth developing economies having 1.39 billion people (UN-POP, 2019) and an average GDP growth rate of 7 percent over the last five years. However, a significant proportion of the population in India is considered to be poor and faces wealth poverty. Around 78 percent of the adult population in India (676 million) earns less than USD 10,000 per annum (CS Global Wealth Report, 2019). This includes around 70.6 million people who are living in extreme poverty and earning less than $1.9 per day (Slater, 2018). The majority of the poor and low-income segment in India is concentrated in the rural areas thereby facing challenges in gaining access to the formal market ecosystem for access to basic needs like food, electricity, shelter, water, loans, insurance, and healthcare (Slater, 2018; Kapoor & Goyal, 2013; Esposito et al., 2012). The similar context at the BoP is prevalent across other developing nations especially in Asia and Africa.

A definitive change in the socioeconomic status of the BoP segment has happened over the years due to CSR initiatives by for-profit businesses, as well as social initiatives and measures by governments, global institutions, and NGOs. However, the change has been slow and driven by the choices of these actors. According to the research literature, socioeconomic change can be faster and more impactful if global businesses target the BoP segment as customers with cocreation–led business models.

This implies that global businesses need to review, assess, and design their product and market strategies as per the needs of the BoP segment rather than relying on the upper- and middle-income segments for their growth and sustainability. On the other hand, global institutions need to formulate goals and initiatives to bridge the socioeconomic gap between the BoP and non-BoP segments, developing and developed economies taking into consideration that future growth and stability requires bridging the socioeconomic inequality between developing and developed nations as well as ensuring a formal market ecosystem for the needs of the BoP segment.

2.2 BoP: Research Literature Overview

The need and urgency for a shift in the global mindset towards the BoP segment concentrated in developing economies is becoming more and more evident in recent research. During 2000–2019, increasing numbers of research articles and publications have been published, highlighting the trends, challenges, differentiated strategies, and social business models targeting the BoP segment across developing economies.

Three broad points of differentiation are evident from the research literature in the context of developed versus developing economies. The first point of differentiation is regarding the socioeconomic profile of the individuals in developing versus developed economies. As discussed, a significant proportion of the population in developing economies belongs to the low- and low-mid income segments, lives in semi-urban and rural areas, and relies on an informal market ecosystem for day-to-day basic needs. The second point relates to relative market opportunity in the developing versus developed economies. Developing economies, especially BRICS nations, are characterized by a positive GDP growth rate, growing infrastructure, growing consumption patterns, and an increasing youth population. This implies that the future scope of business lies in developing economies, especially the low- and low-mid income segments at the BoP. The third point of differentiation is regarding different types of challenges (consumer, market, competitive, infrastructure, and geographic) in the developing versus developed economies. Unlike developed economies, businesses, especially those targeting the BoP segment, need to review, assess, differentiate, and design their business models taking into consideration the socioeconomic limitations, behavioral challenges, and geographic complexities in the developing economies. The fourth point of significance relates to the growing disparity between rich and poor, as well as an overall decline in the count of extreme poor individuals earning less than $1.9 per day. As discussed, the number of people considered to be extreme poor has declined from 1.85 billion in 1990 to 736 million in 2015 (World Bank, 2019).

These developments and trends call for a comprehensive action plan by the governments, development institutions, and commercial and social businesses aimed at targeting the underserved needs of the masses at the BoP via self-sustainable and profitable business models. This has led to the evolution of a separate stream of research literature aimed at understanding the context, opportunities, challenges, and business approach in these emerging economies. Considering the fact that the key market in developing economies corresponds to the BoP segment, research literature emphasizes the need for setting up social businesses that are socioeconomic or environmental-mission focused and drive the social or environmental impact at scale with a for-profit or self-sustainable business model (Prahalad, 2019; Esposito et al., 2012; Porter & Kramer, 2011; Yunus et al., 2010). Porter and Kramer (2011) defined this approach as "Creating Shared Value" comprising three areas of action for businesses aiming for a socioeconomic transformation – reconfiguring the products and markets, redefining productivity in the value chain, and enabling local cluster development. Simultaneously, Yunus et al. (2010) argued that setting up social business is the best way to achieve scale and create socioeconomic or environmental impact at the BoP. Yunus and colleagues defined social business as a non-loss company driven by a social mission. All the profits or surplus revenue generated gets reinvested in the social venture. Investors can claim their money back without any dividend (Cosic, 2017; Yunus et al., 2010).

Shared value and social business orientations are both driven by a social mission and a self-sustainable business model. However, unlike shared value, social business orientation highlights the need for pushing back the profits in scaling the business rather than rewarding the shareholders monetarily.

For the purpose of this research, any self-sustainable or for-profit business or enterprise having a social mission and BoP as a target segment is considered to be in scope and addressed as a social business, irrespective of the reinvestment logic used for the profits.

In this Element, the literature review has focused on a descriptive review of the BoP research articles, especially those articles that have been authored by well-known researchers and published in top peer-reviewed journals. The keywords used for identifying the relevant research articles included base of the pyramid, social businesses, social Infrastructure, social enterprises, IT setup, and bottom of the pyramid. A systemic review of the BoP research literature enabled us to observe and identify its evolution, as well as understand the emergence of different research themes and interpretable research patterns. The following themes have been identified during the literature review: BoP context, segmentation, value proposition or offerings, experimentation and innovation, social embeddedness, networking and collaboration, and scaling (Table 1).

Table 1 BoP literature review: Research themes and subthemes

Main theme	Subthemes
Context	definition, opportunity, needs, challenges
Segmentation	heterogeneity, low-income, subsistence-income, extreme poor
Value offerings	awareness, affordability, acceptability, accessibility, availability, end-to-end solution
Experimentation & innovation	low-cost probes, prototyping, product innovation, process innovation, business-model innovation, embedded innovation paradigm, structural innovation paradigm
Social embeddedness	structural social capital, local engagement, local capacity building
Networking & collaboration	nontraditional partnerships, value cocreation
Scalability	impact, outreach, replication

Source: Authors' compilation

2.2.1 Understanding the Context

Definition and Opportunity

BoP is looked upon as a volatile and uncertain ecosystem, characterized by institutional voids and comprising low-income individuals or households living and transacting in an informal economic setup (Khan, 2016). BoP is a collective reference to around 3.5 billion people belonging to the suboptimal income strata in the world (Prahalad, 2019; CS Global Wealth Report, 2019, 2017). As we have discussed, there has been a significant transformation in overall population numbers and socioeconomic status of the BoP segment during 1990–2019. At one end, global population has grown from 5.2 billion in 1990 to 7.5 billion in 2019 (UNDESA, 2019). A significant proportion of this growth in numbers has taken place in the low-income strata in developing and underdeveloped economies. Another point of significance is the overall decline in numbers at the BoP despite the high rate of population growth in developing economies. The number of people in the BoP segment has seen a decline globally from 4 billion in 2002 to 3.5 billion in 2019 (World Bank, 2019). This count of 3.5 billion includes 736 million people categorized as extreme poor and living on $1.9 per day (World Bank, 2019).

Considering these factors, the BoP segment as a market context has undergone significant transformation between the 1990s and 2019. During early 2000, the BoP segment was defined as a collective reference to around 4 billion people (65 percent of the global population) earning less than $8 per person per day (2002 PPP) (Goyal, Esposito & Kapoor, 2016; Goyal & Sergi, 2015a, 2015b; Goyal, Esposito, Kapoor et al., 2014; Kapoor & Goyal, 2013; Viswanathan & Sridharan, 2012; Esposito et al., 2012; Hammond et al., 2007; Prahalad & Hammond, 2002). By 2017, the BoP segment had undergone a significant shift in terms of overall numbers, count of people in extreme poverty, minimal income levels, and disparity between rich and poor (World Bank, 2019; Prahalad, 2019; CS Global Wealth Report, 2019, 2018, 2017) (Figure 2). During 2000–2019, the rich–poor gap widened with the top 10 percent of the population controlling 82 percent of the overall wealth (CS Global Wealth Report, 2019).

All of these factors signify a mix of positive and negative trends in tackling the global poverty challenge. Poverty has decreased in terms of absolute numbers as well as minimum income tier. Technology penetration, affordability, and accessibility have undergone a significant increase to the last-mile. These are positive indications. However, rich–poor disparity has increased over the same time. Poverty (97 percent of the global poor) is becoming increasingly concentrated in the developing and underdeveloped economies thereby posing a huge challenge for the respective governments and development institutions

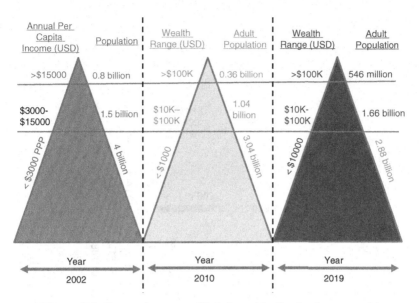

Figure 2 BoP over the years: Global wealth distribution pyramid
(2002, 2010, 2019)

Source: Authors' creation from CS Global Wealth Report (2019, 2010); London (2008); Hammond et al. (2007); Prahalad and Hammond (2004; 2002); Prahalad and Hart (2002)

of these nations. As discussed above, a significant proportion of BoP individuals who are living in extreme poverty reside in regions of Africa and other developing economies like India (Figure 3). Geographically, the majority of BoP individuals are becoming concentrated in Asia-Pacific and sub-Saharan Africa regions. A significant proportion of the BoP population in these regions still earns less than USD 2 per day and lives in extreme poverty (CS Global Wealth Databook, 2018). This is in contrast to the average threshold income levels of the BoP population in Eastern European and LATAM countries (Figure 3).

The desired state of the global income pyramid transforming into a diamond with wealth concentration in the middle still has a long way to go.

These kinds of underlying differences in terms of BoP income thresholds and the growing disparity between rich and poor pose challenges for governments, enterprises, and NGOs in making a right choice of BoP segment, identifying the need to be addressed, and designing the appropriate social business model.

Needs and Challenges

The needs and spending patterns of the BoP segment vary by their income levels. For example, extreme poor households (earning < USD 1 per day per person) spend a major proportion of their earnings on food and depend upon governmental-level

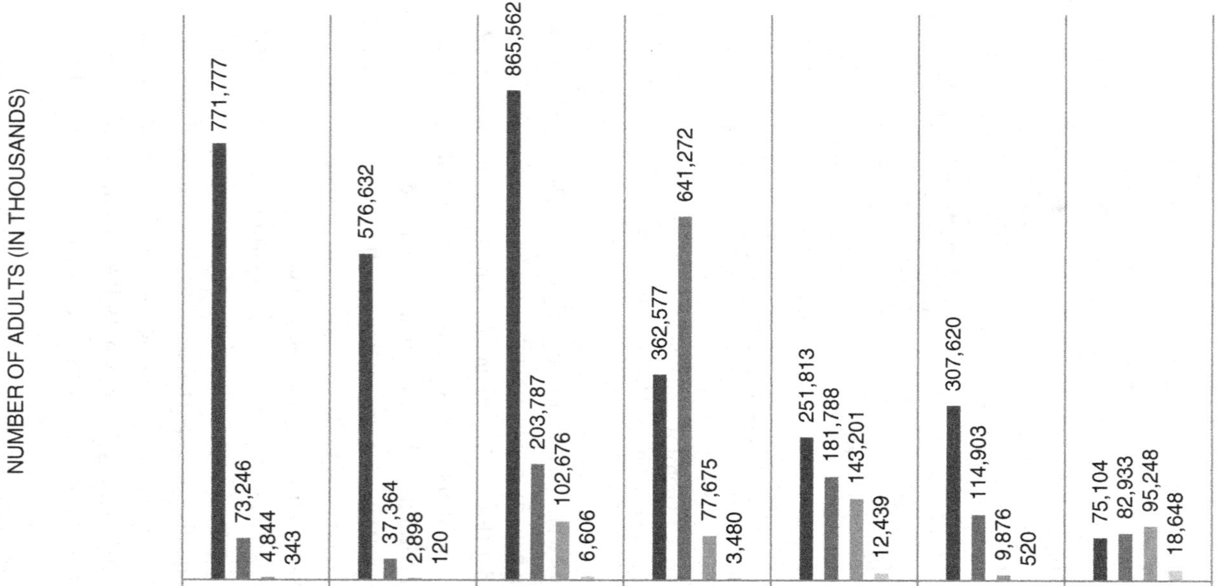

NUMBER OF ADULTS (IN THOUSANDS)	India	Africa	Asia-Pacific	China	Europe	LATAM	N. America
<10K	771,777	576,632	865,562	362,577	251,813	307,620	75,104
10K-100K	73,246	37,364	203,787	641,272	181,788	114,903	82,933
100K-1000K	4,844	2,898	102,676	77,675	143,201	9,876	95,248
>1000K	343	120	6,606	3,480	12,439	520	18,648

Figure 3 Wealth distribution by countries, 2018

Source: Authors' creation from CS Global Wealth Databook (2018)

grants and subsidies for the fulfillment of their basic needs. The BoP segment lacks homogeneity in the sense that the same basic needs hold varying levels of significance for the different sub-income levels at the BoP. The research literature highlights the significance of identifying a particular subsegment within the BoP based upon income level, underserved need, demand-supply situation, level of competition, organizational capacity, and other macro-economic factors. The actions required for operating at the BoP include identifying the unmet basic need, understanding the price point (price-minus rather than cost-plus perspective), and designing and offering the market-based solution for the same.

To be successful at the BoP, enterprises need to look upon the BoP segment as a mix of consumers, producers, micro-entrepreneurs, value cocreators, last-mile employees, or partners rather than as beneficiaries. Despite being a huge opportunity, most for-profit enterprises tend to fail to or decide not to target the BoP segment. Unlike developed economies, there are a diverse set of challenges faced by the enterprises while targeting the BoP segment. The key challenges can be classified into four major categories – customer related, market based, resource oriented, and governance challenges (Sinha & Sheth, 2018, IFMR, 2011). Customer-related challenges involve heterogeneity, low literacy levels, purchase decisions influenced by societal norms and pressure, low-income, irregularity of savings, diversity of languages, limited mobility patterns, and lack of trust in formal market ecosystem. Market-oriented challenges involve low population density, informal competitors, resource scarcity, scarcity of data sets (information and statistical inputs), and infrastructure inadequacy. Resource-oriented challenges involve lack of availability of skilled resources who are willing to make a transition from the high-growth corporate lifestyle to work at the grassroots-level environment in suburban towns and villages with lesser salaries and benefits. Governance-related challenges involve minimal support to commercial enterprises from regional governments in creating awareness among the masses, prevalence of nonproductive and inefficient populist government schemes, and lack of benefits and operational flexibility to the enterprises focusing on the needs of the BoP segment.

Social Entrepreneurship – Rise of Neoliberalism

There has been a gradual rise in neoliberalism with the increasing focus on for-profit business models. Social entrepreneurship is undergoing a shift in focus from underserved needs of the BoP segment to organizational setup and sustainability. There are no doubts regarding the mission-focused setup of for-profit social enterprises at the BoP. However, these for-profit social enterprises are able to target only a specific subsegment of the BoP. Extreme poor are left out of the social business model as self-sustainability gains primary attention followed by the societal needs of the BoP segment. Self-sustainable or for-profit social enterprises focus on scalability and funding just like any other venture capital–funded start-up compared to a grassroots social organization maintaining focus on the underserved needs of the extreme poor (Sharma, Sep 2016). The ideal solution to remaining away from neoliberalism philosophy lies in adoption of a hybrid organizational setup and business model. This implies setting up a combination of for-profit entity and not-for-profit organizational setup. For-profit entity focuses on underserved needs of the paying BoP segment, while not-for-profit organizational setup generates funds from philanthropic sources to serve the underserved needs of extreme poor individuals and households at the BoP. This hybrid combination has proven to be more effective in bringing about social change for the low-income and extreme poor households at the BoP, compared to purely for-profit or not-for-profit entities (Sharma, 2017; 2016). Selco in India is one of the key examples of a hybrid setup at the BoP. Set up in 1995, Selco offers clean energy solutions to BoP households and institutions in rural and semi-urban areas. Selco Solar Lights Pvt. Ltd. is a for-profit setup serving the clean energy needs of the low-income BoP segment residing in rural India that has the ability to pay back in installments. Selco Foundation is a nonprofit setup that generates soft money from philanthropic sources and facilitates access to clean energy solutions for the extreme poor households at the BoP (Goyal et al., 2017).

2.2.2 Segmenting the BoP

The needs and spending patterns of the BoP segment vary as per income level, willingness to pay, and ability to pay. The basis for segmentation involves different factors like living standard (low income, subsistence, and extreme poverty), value creation role (consumers, producers, employees, and clients), and other socioeconomic factors like gender and occupation (Rangan et al., 2011). Due to nonhomogeneity at the BoP, the same needs at the BoP will require differentiated product or service offerings and value-creation strategies for different subsegments. The BoP segment comprises three subsegments primarily on the basis of the income levels: extreme poor (< USD 1/day), subsistence poor (USD 1–3/day), and low-income (USD 3–5/day) (Rangan et al., 2011). **Extreme poor** households spend the major proportion of their income on food, followed by spending on essentials like fuel for cooking and lighting, and health-related issues. This segment remains stuck in the poverty trap and depends mainly on grants and subsidies from the government to survive in day-to-day life. **Subsistence poor** households spend mainly on food items and essentials like energy, healthcare, transportation, and education. This category lacks the paying capacity to spend on discretionary items and remains focused on the fulfillment of its core needs. This category forms a majority of the BoP segment in developing economies like India, China, and Africa. **Low-income poor** spend almost equally on essentials and discretionary items. This category of the BoP segment has the willingness and paying capacity to focus on improving their standard of living by building assets and productive capacity. Pitta et al. (2008) argue that success depends on understanding the BoP intimately. The BoP is a heterogenous segment looking for custom solutions to their specific needs in different geographies. In terms of value-creation strategy, the approach varies from setting up direct distribution channels to building commercial partnerships with nontraditional partners at the BoP. The varying options include targeting the low-income segment by setting up direct distribution channels, the subsistence income segment by engaging CBOs and locals for creating awareness and distribution of offerings, and the extreme poor segment by collaborating with the government and NGOs (Rangan et al., 2011).

2.2.3 Understand the Underserved Needs and Provide Need-Based Value Offerings

The research literature highlights the significance of choice and type of product or service offerings at the BoP.

Prahalad (2004) has been a pioneer in generating renewed interest and focus of commercial enterprises and academicians towards the underserved needs and potential opportunities at the BoP. He defined the BoP segment as a large proportion of the low-income population lacking access to affordable, accessible, and optimal quality value offerings for their basic needs. The BoP segment remains dependent upon the informal economy due to a lack of focus by commercial enterprises in developing a formal market ecosystem where affordable products and services are offered as per the real needs of the low-income segment. The prevalence of inefficient local monopolies, inadequate access, poor distribution, and strong traditional middlemen has led to the continuation of a vicious poverty cycle for the BoP (Prahalad, 2004). The vicious circle of poverty penalty has remained as one of the biggest constraints for the socioeconomic advancement of the BoP segment. Hammond et al. (2007) demonstrate the existence of a poverty penalty: *"Many in the BoP, and perhaps most, pay higher prices for basic goods and services than do wealthier consumers – either in cash or in the effort they must expend to obtain them – and they often receive lower quality as well."*

Viswanathan et al. (2008) argue that providing value offerings at the BoP involves design of products or services that enable engagement of the BoP segment not only as customers but also as employees, distributors, and suppliers. Successful enterprises at the BoP focus on the value creation and offerings at the BoP, wherein the low-income segment can be involved in different roles of consumer, producer, micro-entrepreneur, employee, etc., thereby capturing both demand and source sides of the economic activity (Karnani, 2007). Eyring et al. (2011) have described value offering or customer value proposition (CVP) as a need-based solution that must solve the real need more effectively, simply, accessibly, and affordably than the available alternatives. Affordability and accessibility are considered to be the key components of CVP (Eyring et al., 2011).

Socioeconomic transition of BoP segment needs focus on design of value offerings that can eliminate the vicious circle of poverty penalty. This implies design of product and service offerings that are affordable, accessible, available, and socially acceptable. Moreover, business enterprises need to invest time and effort on market building and creating awareness (market information, details of product/service offering).

Awareness

Britz (2004) has defined lack of awareness or information poverty as a situation in which individuals and communities do not possess requisite skills, abilities, or material means to gain efficient access to information, interpret it meaningfully, and apply it appropriately. Lack of awareness results in a situation of disadvantage for low-income people while dealing with the different stakeholders and makes them feel powerless and dependent upon informal-market players (Narayan et al., 2000). Information scarcity and asymmetry act as major constraints for the BoP segment while trying to make a transition towards the formal market ecosystem. Setting up an ecosystem for market building and awareness generates trust, improves transaction governance, and enhances acceptance among the BoP segment. For example, healthcare social enterprise Aravind Eyecare sets up regular eye camps in the villages to establish a deep connection with the poor people as well as to educate them regarding the significance of pre-screening eye checkups and restoration of vision.

Affordability

Successful enterprises at the BoP have designed their value offerings in accordance with the willingness and ability to pay of the target segment. Those product or service offerings exhibiting a high performance-to-price ratio have a greater chance of adoption at the BoP level than cheaper offerings with low performance and quality (Prahalad, 2006; 2004). Affordability of the product or service solutions at the BoP is determined based on the cost-benefit ratio for the consumer. According to Pitta et al. (2008), BoP consumers are willing to adopt branded products if available in an economy range with sustained quality levels. Similarly, Eyring et al. (2011) stress upon the need for cost-focus strategy and provisioning of mandatory features or attributes in product or service offerings at the BoP.

Acceptability

There is a need for value offerings that are in synchronization with the social norms and values at the BoP. The choices and buying behavior of BoP individuals are influenced by societal approval. The BoP segment lives and transacts in an informal economy and therefore maintains a lack of trust in commercial enterprises: for-profit enterprises are exploitative, lacking personal access and engagement (Banerjee & Duflo, 2007; Letelier et al., 2003). This makes it imperative for enterprises to comply with social norms and expectations. Another aspect that needs attention, is regarding the social comfort level of the BoP segment in accepting the value proposition. This includes managing feelings of loneliness, fear, social implications, and self-doubt (Chambers, 1997). One of the ways to build trust and acceptance involves increasing the level of engagement with the local population beyond entering into partnerships with the local NGOs (London & Hart, 2004; Letelier et al., 2003; Chambers, 1997).

Accessibility and Availability

Nonavailability of last-mile channels for distribution of product or service offerings is one of the key challenges at the BoP, especially in semi-urban and rural areas (Jose, 2008; Prahalad, 2004). Due to limited cash flow and need for daily earnings, the BoP segment is driven by the urgency of a particular need while buying anything. So, successful enterprises need to ensure availability as per the working and mobility patterns of the BoP segment (Jose, 2008; Prahalad, 2004). Pitta et al. (2008) argue that last-mile channels for distribution and delivery need to ensure geographical and emotional proximity to the BoP segment. This implies setting up a sales and distribution channel that is adaptive to the needs and flexible as per the mobility patterns of the BoP segment. Last-mile accessibility and adaptive availability ensures trust and acceptance at the BoP.

Solution-Based Offerings

Due to limited cash flow, BoP individuals look for product or service offerings that can be customized as per their needs and paying capacity. Moreover, BoP individuals are interested in those product or service offerings that meet their aspirational value, are customizable as per their paying capacity, are financially affordable, and involve a high range of usability, durability, and after-sales support (Jose, 2008b; Pitta et al., 2008; Grootaert et al., 2004; Prahalad, 2004; Letelier et al., 2003). Offering a stand-alone product or service lacks sufficient interest and adoption at the BoP (Jose, 2008b; Pitta et al., 2008). Aspirational value of a value offering implies how the target segment conceives possibilities in life, happiness, pride, energy levels, and personal efficacy by adopting the product or service (Grootaert et al., 2004; Letelier et al., 2003). For example, Selco, a social enterprise engaged in providing energy solutions at the BoP in India, offers end-to-end solutions, which include customized product offerings, door-step financing, and door-step servicing (Goyal et al., 2017; Goyal, Esposito, Kapoor, et al., 2014). The energy solutions are customized as per the income level, housing type, and paying capacity of the BoP individuals.

2.2.4 Focus on Experimentation and Innovation

Successful enterprises at the BoP attribute the significant role of experimentation and grassroots innovation to identifying the right product or service offerings as per the real needs of the BoP segment. Scarcity of market and customer-related information, infrastructure challenges, availability of limited cash flow, and scarcity of skilled resources make it important for the enterprises to focus on continuous experimentation and innovation before full-scale launch of value offerings.

Experimentation

Simanis and Hart (2006) argue that enterprises need to focus on continuous field-based learning, low-cost probes, flexible resource allocation, and organizational setup to gain clarity in regard to the right solutions for the needs of the BoP segment. The series of low-cost probes or prototyping minimize the risk of failures and maximize the rate of learning, thereby improving the chances of finding the right solutions for the BoP segment (Yunus et al., 2010; Simanis & Hart, 2006). Focus on experimentation enables the enterprises to develop the ability to adapt and respond to the dynamic environment at the BoP (Yunus et al., 2010).

Innovation

Innovation is another related attribute required for the success of enterprises at the BoP. Successful businesses at the BoP attribute their success to the combination of product, process, and business model innovation. One of the key enablers for developing innovation capacity is access to information at the grassroots level. This requires developing native capability, which involves a dynamic ability to *"systematically identify, explore, and integrate the views of stakeholders on the fringe"* (Hart & Sharma, 2004) as well as the capacity to codiscover and cocreate new value offerings, value creation, and delivery models with the local engagement of marginalized groups and communities (Simanis et al., 2008; Hart, 2005; Hart & London, 2005; Hart & Sharma, 2004).

Besides access to grassroots information, process innovation requires systemic orientation for idea generation, evaluation, and value cocreation (McGrath, 2010; London, 2009; Hart & Sharma, 2004). Technology plays a significant role in the creation of unique product or service offerings as well as design and implementation of the innovative business models at the BoP (Chesbrough, 2010; Teece, 2010; Hart & Christensen, 2002).

Andersen and Markides (2007) argue that innovation at the BoP has less to do with finding new customers than addressing the 5A's (awareness, affordability, accessibility, availability, and acceptance) challenges. Scarcity of capital and controlled cash flow require the enterprises to implement asset-light business models at the BoP (Jose, 2008a; Prahalad & Ramaswamy, 2006).

Simanis and Hart (2009) highlight two distinct innovation paradigms, which yield varying results in different markets. The first is the Structural Innovation Paradigm (SIP), which involves the adoption of a short-term, transaction-oriented approach for delivering products or services that are cheaper, better, and faster than the ones by the competitors in the market. The second is the Embedded Innovation Paradigm (EIP), which focuses on business intimacy driven by closeness and mutual commitment of firm and target community. This involves transformational engagement of the stakeholders leading to relationship-based value and holds greater relevance for the BoP markets.

2.2.5 Focus on Social Embeddedness

The research literature emphasizes the need for social embeddedness on the part of enterprises to build trust and transparency at the BoP, as well as to collect reliable local market inputs for design of need-based solutions.

Structural social capital rather than legal contracts holds greater significance and relevance for businesses in gaining acceptance at the BoP (London & Hart, 2004; Grootaert & Van, 2002; Soto, 2000; Granovetter, 1985). Structural social capital involves *"developing the norms and networks that enable people [and organizations] to act collectively"* (Grootaert & Van, 2002; Woolcock & Narayan, 2000). Focus on social capital enables businesses to develop resource capacity and buffer against market uncertainty, besides reducing transaction costs and risks. Trust and transparency are considered to be the cognitive dimensions of social capital and play an important role in the success of businesses at the BoP (Goyal & Sergi, 2015a; Goyal, Esposito & Kapoor, 2014). The low-income segment at the BoP can be won over by investing in social capital rather than creating legal contracts. There are increasing numbers of businesses at the BoP focusing on developing their global capability in social embeddedness.

Social embeddedness is defined as the engagement of an organization operating at the BoP with the local community not only for business transactions but also as a long-term relationship (London & Hart, 2004). It is also defined as *"the extent to which a company's strategy reflects or is influenced by its social and institutional connections"* (Miller, 1996).

Social embeddedness involves lifting the psychological and cultural barriers; developing local capacity and developing a local presence within people's everyday lives. In the BoP context, local capacity building is defined as *"interaction of human capital, organizational resources, and social capital existing within a given community that can be leveraged to solve collective problems and improve and maintain the well-being of that community"* (Chaskin et al., 2001).

The key actions for local capacity building involve training and engaging local individuals as employees, micro-entrepreneurs, and suppliers (Gibb & Adhikary, 2000); building nontraditional partnerships with informal market players and NGOs (Hart & London, 2005; Hart, 2005); setting up a localized learning ecosystem at the grassroots level; enabling access to information and communication technologies like mobile and internet; and promoting value cocreation with the locals at the BoP (Esposito et al., 2012). The localized learning ecosystem involves a systemic process for identifying, exploring, and integrating the views of the fringe stakeholders that leads to the design and implementation of sustainable business models comprising local engagement of marginalized groups and communities (Hart & Sharma, 2004).

2.2.6 Networking and Collaboration: Nontraditional Partners

Prevalence of an informal economy ecosystem is one of the key challenges for enterprises targeting the BoP segment. As discussed before, the BoP segment lives and transacts in an informal economy characterized by increasingly prevalent market imperfections like information asymmetry, weak legal institutional setup, market fragmentation, weak infrastructure, constrained availability of resources, and a poverty penalty (Viswanathan et al., 2007). Market imperfections and environmental complexities lead to higher transaction costs and entry barriers for enterprises at the BoP.

To address these market imperfections and transaction costs, enterprises need to focus on developing the market-based ecosystem comprising strong partnerships with NGOs, CBOs, local institutions, the local population, informal market competitors, and government bodies (Goyal & Sergi, 2015; Goyal et al., 2015; Hart, 2005; London & Hart, 2004; Prahalad, 2004; Prahalad & Hart, 2002). Successful nontraditional partnerships at the grassroots level are driven by focusing on social capital rather than aiming for legal contracts (Hart, 2005; London & Hart, 2004; Soto, 2000).

Prahalad (2004) describes collaboration and networking as an ecosystem comprising a variety of institutions complementing each other. Collaboration involves bringing together private enterprises, government institutions, NGOs, CBOs, and local market competitors to cocreate value at the BoP. Hart (2005) points out that nontraditional partnerships with local institutions and individuals enable enterprises to gain local trust and acceptance, optimize transaction costs, reduce entry barriers, develop local channels for distribution and delivery, as well as gain deep understanding of local needs. Dahan and colleagues (2010) highlight the significance of collaboration with NGOs in the success of business models at the BoP. Win-win partnerships between commercial enterprises and NGOs require complementary skills and resources, trust building, shared goals and objectives, and understanding of the local context.

2.3 BoP: Literature Review Findings and Directions

The review of research literature indicates growing significance of BoP as a viable market proposition. A growing number of enterprises and government institutions are looking at the BoP segment differently. No longer is the BoP a pure-play setup driven by grants, donations, and philanthropy. Since the launch of United Nations Millennium Development Goals (UN MDGs) in 2010,[3] no developing nation wants to be known as an anti-poor or insensitive nation where a significant proportion of the citizens live and transact in an informal market ecosystem. Although informal market ecosystem is still prevalent to a greater or lesser extent in the developing nations, these nations are consistently taking action towards improving the socioeconomic welfare and situation of the BoP segment. Let's consider the example of China.

According to World Bank estimates, 90 percent of the people in China were extreme poor (< USD 2 per person per day) in 1978.[4] The poverty scenario changed by 2014, when more than 95 percent of the population in China moved above the extreme poverty line. Multiple initiatives were taken by successive

---

[3] www.un.org/millenniumgoals/bkgd.shtml (last accessed 29 June 2019).
[4] www.telegraph.co.uk/china-watch/society/decreasing-chinas-poverty/ (last accessed 29 June 2019).

Chinese governments, like driving entrepreneurship at the grassroots level, enabling access to basic infrastructure (like roads, drinking water, electricity, housing, financing, insurance, healthcare, etc.) in semi-urban towns and villages, launching awareness-building programs in villages, leveraging digital technologies and platforms for enabling last-mile access, and inclusion of the BoP segment in various benefits and programs.

During 1990–2020, similar actions, albeit with different levels of success, have been initiated in other developing nations to move more and more people above the poverty line. The review of academic literature brings forth an evolutionary pattern in terms of mindset and strategies adopted by different nations in targeting the BoP segment over the years. The evolutionary phenomenon and mindset can be analyzed across three phases – **BoP 1.0, BoP 2.0, and BoP 3.0**.

BoP 1.0 or the first-generation BoP phase points to the timeframe beginning in the mid-twenieth century wherein the majority of the pro-poor stakeholders, like enterprises, governments, development institutions, and NGOs, etc., have looked upon the BoP segment as a beneficiary and targeted them by offering free or cheap products and services. The majority of the needs of the BoP segment are addressed via CSR initiatives of the enterprises, public policy initiatives and grants by the government, and social initiatives by the NGOs and CBOs. From the viewpoint of private enterprises, serving the needs of the BoP segment does not yield economic returns and needs to be taken care of by government and NGOs. BoP1.0 strategies have achieved limited success in bringing about a sustainable improvement in the lives of the poor due to the common perception of BoP segment as beneficiaries rather than consumers.

BoP 2.0 or the second-generation BoP phase started gaining ground in the late 1990s due to two big ideas that challenged the dominant mindset and strategies being used for addressing the needs of the poor.

The **first** idea involves the introduction of term "BoP" when Prahalad and Hart (2002) introduced the concept of BoP as a radical idea of looking at 4 billion poor globally in the form of a huge socioeconomic opportunity. According to Prahalad, these 4 billion poor people, also tagged as the BoP segment, present a huge market opportunity for enterprises in the form of grassroots partners, value cocreators, micro-entrepreneurs, consumers, suppliers, and employees. This idea challenged long-held assumptions regarding the role of government, development institutions, NGOs, and enterprises in addressing the needs of the poor (Prahalad, 2019).

The second idea relates to the increasing focus on social entrepreneurship or social enterprises (SE) as a new way of doing business at the BoP. Research literature highlights two broad conceptions of SEs. The original and dominant conception of SEs involves those enterprises that are driven by "serve" or "social change" mindsets irrespective of economic returns or sustainability (Dees, 2017; Goyal, Sergi, & Jaiswal, 2016; Goyal et al., 2015; Chell, 2007; Tracey & Phillips, 2007; Austin et al., 2006). These enterprises attract human and resource capital having community-spirited and social welfare motives, and rely on donations, philanthropic funding, and government subsidies and grants to fulfill their social mission. However, during the beginning of the twenty-first century, the idea and meaning of social enterprise has expanded beyond representation by nonprofit organizational entities to represent self-sustainable or for-profit organization entities targeting social needs. The new conception of SEs involves those enterprises, which are driven by "serve and survive" or "socioeconomic change" perspectives (Goyal, Sergi, & Jaiswal, 2016; Goyal et al., 2015; London, 2008; Ridley-Duff, 2008; Chell, 2007; Tracey & Phillips, 2007; Austin et al., 2006; Peredo & McLean, 2006; London & Hart, 2004; Dees & Anderson, 2003). These enterprises design and implement for-profit, innovative, and market-based business models for maximizing the social impact and economic returns. In these enterprises, success is measured on the basis of their social impact, outreach levels, scalability, and revenue streams. To summarize, the latest trend of for-profit SEs involves design and implementation of innovative business models that blend the market efficiencies of commercial enterprises and the last-mile capabilities (promotion and delivery) of NGOs to design value offerings, and a creation and delivery network at the BoP (Goyal, Sergi, & Jaiswal, 2016; Goyal & Sergi, 2015b; Luke and Chu, 2013).

The binding theme in both definitions of SEs involves belief and practice towards "serve" philosophy (Figure 4). What economic model is being followed to bring out a positive social change at the BoP? This determines the organizational setup and strategies. However, the self-sustainable entrepreneurial approach, driven by a "serve and survive" philosophy, is gaining recognition as a better way of addressing poverty as compared to the "serve" approach or the "survive" mindset.

The review of BoP research literature brings forth the following key focus areas (KFAs), which play a significant role in the success and sustainability of for-profit SEs at the BoP – solution-based offerings, value cocreation, local capacity building, experimentation and innovation driven by grassroots learning-based ecosystem, and nontraditional partnerships. Strategic actions linked to solution-based offerings involve design of end-to-end solutions in accordance with the real need, willingness to pay (WTP), and ability to pay (ATP) of the BoP target segment. Value cocreation involves targeting and engaging BoP individuals not only as consumers

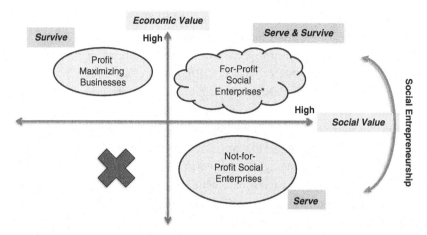

Figure 4 Entrepreneurial approach at the BoP

Source: Authors' creation

but also as producers, suppliers, employees, and micro-entrepreneurs across the product or service value chain. Local capacity building (LCB) involves actions aimed at promoting awareness, enhancing market-based skills of the locals by holding training camps, and engaging local individuals for last-mile connectivity and reach as suppliers, micro-entrepreneurs, and employees. Nontraditional collaborations and partnerships involve forming win-win associations with development institutions, local competitors, government institutions, NGOs, and CBOs to gain trust and acceptance as well as to leverage their last-mile channels and distribution network at the BoP. Experimentation and innovation involves building community-level engagement to gain understanding of the real needs of the BoP segment as well as conducting low-cost probes and field-pilots before full-scale launch of any value offering at the BoP.

BoP 3.0 or the third-generation BoP phase relates to the transformative period after first decade of the twenty-first century when digital technologies, circular economy, and innovative funding models, along with collaborations and networking, emerged as significant enablers in restoring the ecological balance, maximizing the socioeconomic impact at the BoP, as well as providing sustainability and scalability to social businesses (Chmielewski et al., 2018; Goyal et al., 2016).

Digital technologies are undergoing rapid advancement, adoption, and penetration among organizations and individuals globally. The growth rate and penetration of digital technologies is among the highest in developing economies like Africa and India, especially in semi-urban and rural regions (Spence et al., 2010). Ease of connectivity, along with affordable access to mobiles and internet technologies, are being valued as a significant value-add by the BoP segment for the socioeconomic transformation of their lives.

Circular economy (CEC) is another key driver that is gaining ground as a restorative mechanism to stretch the availability and usage of natural resources. According to the Ellen MacArthur Foundation (EMF), CEC is defined as an upstream, closed-loop approach that is regenerative and restorative by design. CEC involves moving away from a consumption-based orientation towards minimizing waste generation by emphasizing the active use and extended life cycle of products, materials, and resources (Goyal, 2019; Geisendorf & Pietrulla, 2018; UNEP, 2018). According to United Nations Sustainable Development Goals (UN SDGs) (2016), there is an impending ecological disaster due to widening demand–supply gap for natural resources. The population on this planet will reach beyond 8 billion in 2030 and 9.3 billion in 2050, requiring two and three planets worth of natural resources respectively (McCarthy, 2017). This makes it imperative for everybody to transform the value chain and consumption model from the use-and-throw oriented linear approach (take-make-dispose) towards a circular approach (reduce, recycle, and reuse).

Social financial engineering is considered to be another key factor in growth and sustainability of social businesses. However, the social-financial gap between potential returns and needed investments in addressing basic needs at the BoP remains a perennial challenge for social businesses as the majority of investors look at the potential returns as a criterion for making any investments.

There are innovative funding models coming up to mentor and incubate those early-stage social businesses having the potential to bring about a positive transformation in the lives of the poor (Bugg-Levine et al., 2012). Table 2 highlights the evolutionary view of the BoP landscape.

A detailed review of the research literature, especially **BoP 3.0**, highlights the increasing role of smart social infrastructures including digital technologies, partnerships, networking, social financial engineering, and innovative business models in maximizing the socioeconomic and environmental impact at the BoP. These learnings from the literature review become the basis for deeper-level analysis while looking at social businesses. The next section will establish the research methodology and identify a sample of those social businesses in India that have leveraged smart social infrastructures in achieving a significant level of scalability and sustainability at the BoP.

Table 2 BoP landscape and strategies: Evolutionary view

	BoP1.0	BoP2.0	BoP3.0
Recognition period	Mid 20th century	Late 1990s	Year 2010 onwards
BoP segment	Beneficiary	Value cocreator[1]	Value cocreator[1]
Mission	Serve	Serve and Survive	Serve and survive
What kind of relationship at BoP?	Transaction based	Relationship based – Local engagement and social embeddedness	Relationship based – Local engagement and social embeddedness
Organizational Types	Nonprofits, government, csr/philanthropic, NGOs	Social enterprises (Nonprofit, for-profit, hybrid), csr, ngos, government	Social enterprises (Nonprofit, for-profit, hybrid), csr, ngos, government
Key drivers (Organizational level)	Self-consciousness, societal responsibility, social branding	Realization of unmet socioeconomic opportunity, social entrepreneurship, Prahalad's BoP concept, competitive branding	UN SDGs, social and technology infrastructure, circular economies, social financial engineering
Role of technology	Low	Medium	High
Business model typologies	social	Self-sustainable	Disruptive

[1] Prosumer, micro-entrepreneur, last-mile sales, customer services, micro-franchisee

Source: Authors' compilation

3 Research Methodology, Sampling, and Data Collection

This Element involves understanding the types and role of "smart" social infrastructures in BoP emerging markets like India. The question here is that why India has been selected as a region for this research. As explained previously, India accounts for around 700 million people earning less than USD 10,000 per annum (CS Global Wealth Report, 2019; 2018). This is the largest proportion of people lying at the BoP in any single country (Figure 3). Moreover, India is one of the leading economies in terms of GDP growth rate and overall population numbers. Both these factors imply a significant role for India as a market context for understanding the design and implementation of social business models at the BoP.

To address this objective, it is required to identify and analyze those social businesses that have integrated the "smart" social innovations like digital technologies, partnerships/networking, and social financial engineering in their core business model. From here onwards, such of businesses will be referred to as successful social businesses.

A detailed level of qualitative multicase-based research methodology has been adopted to understand the complexities, challenges, and strategic actions taken by the successful social businesses. The case study approach is preferable to the survey or experimental approach in those situations where there is a need to maintain a holistic perspective during data collection and analysis of real-life events throughout the study (Yin, 2009). There are many historical pieces of evidence in research and practitioner-based studies, which highlight the significant role of interactive paradigm and case-based research in understanding a particular phenomenon.

This Element adopts a mix of deductive-inductive research logic and applies the grounded theory research method for problem formulation, data collection, and data analysis. The deductive stage aims at identifying a broad list of categories/focus areas, which are evident in the research literature. These categories/focus areas act as a broad framework for the subsequent inductive stage of this research. This ensures that the researcher can focus, sort, and structure data in an informative manner during the qualitative research (Miles, 1979). During the deductive phase, focus will be on identifying a sample list of social businesses that are making use of a combination of one or more key drivers identified in BoP 3.0.

This will be followed by an inductive stage, when an interpretive epistemological approach is applied to the selected list of social businesses to review and establish key drivers (key success factors) needed for the success of social businesses at the BoP.

The intent of this Element is inductive theory building, being subjected to recursive iterations between data collection, data analysis, emergent theory, and extant literature. Eisenhardt describes this approach of simultaneous data collection and analysis as **"controlled opportunism."** The objective of inductive theory-building logic is to create theory from an interpretive epistemological approach applied via a qualitative case-based approach (Eisenhardt & Melissa, 2007).

One of the key considerations in a case-study approach involves focus on theoretical sampling. The case-based theory-building research relies on theoretical sampling, which involves making a choice of the cases on the basis of theoretical, not statistical, reasons (Glaser & Strauss, 1967). The cases are chosen to replicate previous cases or extend the emergent theory, or they may be chosen to fill theoretical categories and provide examples of polar types (Eisenhardt, 1989).

The selection of social businesses or social enterprises gets complicated by the fact that the term "social" or "inclusive" means different things to different people, depending on their personal and cultural backgrounds. Which social needs should have priority? This ambiguity is resolved by selecting those social businesses that are targeting those social needs at the BoP, which are linked to UN SDGs. These goals are designed to set up the priority focus areas as well as to secure the commitment of global institutions and businesses with the objective of achieving sustainable development (Seelos & Mair, 2005).

The following methodology has been used while selecting a sample of social businesses in the scope of this Element:

- Formed a panel of practitioners and academicians having experience or expertise to a certain extent in social entrepreneurial ecosystems.
- Set up meetings and interactions with the expert panel for deciding upon an optimal approach/criterion to make a selection of social businesses. The criteria evaluated social businesses on the following points:
  > Based out of India and been set up in the twenty-first century
  > Operational in India for at least two years before the start of this research
  > Offers product or service solutions at the BoP, which are aligned with the UN SDGs
  > Follows a self-sustainable or profitable or hybrid business model rather than relying solely on grants and donations
  > Showcases significant socioeconomic or environmental impact at the BoP
  > Uses smart digital technologies while targeting the underserved needs of the BoP segment in India

Table 3 highlights the sample list of social businesses that have been selected based upon the specified criteria. Moreover, an attempt has been made to ensure the coverage of need segments, where smart social

Table 3 Sampling details: Social businesses/ enterprises

Enterprise	Year of start	Need addressed	Impact
Villgro	2001	Incubate social enterprises to build innovative, scalable, sustainable, and profitable solutions for societal needs at the BoP.	**To Dec 2018:** More than 250 impactful social enterprises in agribusiness, education, employability, healthcare, and renewable energy.
Aavishkaar	2001	Incubate social entrepreneurs targeting BoP needs with impact investing and mentoring.	**To Dec 2018:** 55 portfolio enterprises; >70 million lives impacted and created 150,000 jobs; >USD 200 million assets.
Rang De	2006	Low-cost access to micro-credit for micro-entrepreneurs from poor communities.	**To Jul 2019:** 14,000 investors; 65,000 loans; INR 759 million disbursement; 93.64 percent repayment rate.
Phool	2015	Recycling flower waste from temples into incense, vermicompost, and biodegradable packaging material thereby providing sustainable livelihoods to poor women employed in recycling and preventing water and soil pollution.	**To Dec 2018:** 11,060 tons flowers recycled; 75 BOP women employed; 11 tons pesticide off-set; 19 children from BoP families in school.
Let's Recycle (Nepra Resource Management)	2012	Setting up organized win-win dry-waste supply chain connecting waste generators, informal waste collectors, and recyclers.	**To Dec 2018:** 5,000+ waste pickers at BoP; 500+ waste generators; ~25,000 Metric Tonnes (MT) waste diverted from landfill; >32,000 MT CO_2 savings.

Table 3 (cont.)

Enterprise	Year of start	Need addressed	Impact
Sarvajal (Piramal Water Pvt. Ltd.)	2008	Leveraging technology to bring community-level safe and affordable drinking water solutions to the underserved segment.	**To Jul 2019:** 632,000 consumers served daily across 19 states in India; >1,005 purification units; >575 water automatic vending machines (ATMs); locals engaged as micro-entrepreneurs; >955 million liters water served.
GARV Toilets	2015	Providing smart, accessible, and affordable solutions to water, sanitation, and hygiene needs of the underserved segment.	**To Jan 2019:** 4 countries, >721 installations; >300,000 services per day; 102.4 tons CO_2 reduction annually.
BEMPU	2014	Launched an intuitive, neonatal temperature-monitoring device to better manage newborn babies' health.	**To Jan 2019:** 14,862 newborns reached; 266 lives saved; 725 health workers empowered; 135 facilities using BEMPU.
Janitri	2017	Launched an affordable, easy-to-use, and portable uterine contraction monitoring device for low-resources healthcare settings thereby saving maternal and newborn lives.	**To Jan 2019:** 111 hospitals; 22,130 pregnancies covered; 8 states in India.

Note: INCB: Incubator/Incubatee; Fin Engg: Social Financial Engineering – Impact/Crowdfunding; Tech: Leverage Technology; NW: Networking/ Collaboration; CE: Circular Economy

Source: Authors' creation – Websites of select enterprises

infrastructure plays an important role for delivering high-impact value offerings at the BoP. The choice of social businesses continued until a stage of theoretical saturation was reached in terms of findings. Theoretical saturation is defined as the threshold point at which the incremental learning is minimal due to the similarity of the phenomenon to the prior learning (Glaser & Strauss, 1967).

4 Social Businesses Overview

4.1 Villgro

The power of innovation, combined with entrepreneurship, to impact the lives of the people who are poor.

– **Paul Basil, Founder, Villgro**

Mission

Villgro is driven by a mission of creating innovative, impactful, self-sustainable, and successful social enterprises.

What Is the Underlying Context and Background?

To 2001, social entrepreneurship, impact investing, and incubation were little known as means for creating scalable social impact at the BoP in India. Paul Basil identified a huge gap between the underserved needs of the BoP segment and available market-based solutions to serve those needs. The need for making a push towards scalable, replicable, and self-sustainable market-based solutions to address the socioenvironmental issues and needs of the BoP segment led Basil to set up Villgro in 2001 (VIR, 2018). Rather than setting up a social enterprise to address the specific need of the BoP segment, Paul decided to build an ecosystem that could inspire, incubate, motivate, and engage innovators and social entrepreneurs to move beyond an early-idea stage towards a self-sustainable and high-impact business model. Over the years, an increasing number of start-ups have realized the significance of on-ground operational and financial support to build sustainable business models to solve the underserved social needs of the BoP segment in developing economies like India (Team YS, Aug 2019).

Srinivas Ramanujam, Chief Operating Officer, Villgro said, *"Incubators need to become the go-to place for social impact startups to find that kind of support."* (Team YS, Aug 2019)

Understanding the Socioeconomic Impact

Between 2001 and 2019, Villgro incubated 279 innovators into mission-driven, scalable, and self-sustainable social enterprises. It has raised more than INR 1,796 million investment capital and INR 573 million as seed funding. During the nineteen years of its journey from 2001 to 2018, Villgro's ecosystem has created more than 3,500 skilled jobs and impacted the lives of more than 19 million people at the BoP to date (Villgro Website, 2019). Villgro has replicated the incubation model to support social enterprises in Kenya, Philippines, and Vietnam.

How Does It Operate?

Villgro is driven by a belief that scale and impact at the BoP is possible only when organizations move away from traditional forms of charity towards a self-sustainable business model where poor and marginalized individuals at the BoP are engaged as value cocreators. The company provides an end-to-end ecosystem for early-stage social entrepreneurs from inspiration to investment via four pillars – **Unconvention, iPitch, Villgro, and Menterra.** Unconvention inspires, iPitch discovers, Villgro incubates, and Menterra invests in the ideas having a potential for high socioeconomic impact and scale at the BoP (Villgro Website, 2019).

iPitch is an annual discovering platform that invites and shortlists high-impact potential ideas in the areas of agritech, medtech, edutech, cleantech, livelihood, skill building, and employability. Villgro evaluates and shortlists the social enterprises every year on the basis of simplicity of the innovation; ubiquity of the underserved need among the target segment; early traction and strong validation; and finally, mission and passion of the founders (Bhalla, Aug 2019).

This is followed by **Unconvention**, which is a confluence of diverse stakeholders in the field of social entrepreneurship, including CSR heads, policy makers, investors, and social entrepreneurs who come together to discuss, share, inspire, and partner with each other for creating high-impact business solutions at the BoP. The scope of discussion involves mainly underserved needs related to agri-business, energy, healthcare, education, employability, and environment faced by the BoP segment in India.

Next comes the **Incubation phase**, which involves a range of activities as follows. The first step involves setting up a diagnostic panel to review and assess the business idea, mission, governance, scalability approach, and business model. The second step involves laying down a one-hundred-day incubation plan to enable alignment of the company's long-term goals with short-term deliverables. The third step involves identifying a technical advisory having expertise in launching a start-up in the respective business domain and associating this person with the entrepreneur to support him/her in solution development, intellectual property filing strategy, and freedom-to-operate model. Then comes the human resource advisory for developing a core team and a financial advisory to develop the fundraising strategy, building a pitch-deck, and identifying potential investors. The final activity involves finalizing a go-to-market strategy to help in market assessment, clinical trials or pilots, and regulatory compliance. This integrated incubation ecosystem has enabled Villgro to incubate novel impact ideas into a meaningful value proposition supported by a self-sustainable business model.

For example, Villgro has incubated an Internet of Things (IoT) start-up, which has reduced the price of automating drip irrigation by 90 percent. This has made the technology affordable for the masses at the BoP as well as expanded the market opportunity by eight times for a large irrigation equipment manufacturer (Ramanujam, May 2019). Similarly, Villgro has been involved with a telemedicine start-up that has developed a technology-enabled pathology lab that does not need skilled operators for MRI and radiology machines. This has enabled a leading medical equipment brand to expand its sales and reach into tier-II cities (Ramanujam, May 2019). Figure 5 provides a detailed overview regarding Villgro's business model.

4.2 Aavishkaar

The biggest challenge is not in finding the entrepreneur or the innovation but in providing the risk capital. We believe in making investments in distressed or difficult areas. If world changes in the process, that is great.
— **Vineet Rai, Founder, Aavishkaar** (Meghani, Jan 2018)

Vision

To catalyze equitable development globally by supporting entrepreneurial intervention through provision of risk capital.

Mission

To evolve an approach to investing that nurtures entrepreneurs in building enterprises that can generate commercial returns while serving humanity sustainably.

What Is the Underlying Context and Background?

The seeds of Aavishkaar were sown in the mind of Vineet Rai in 1998, when he joined Grassroots Innovation Augmentation Network (GIAN) as a CEO. GIAN was set up in 1997 by the Gujarat Government as an incubator to support

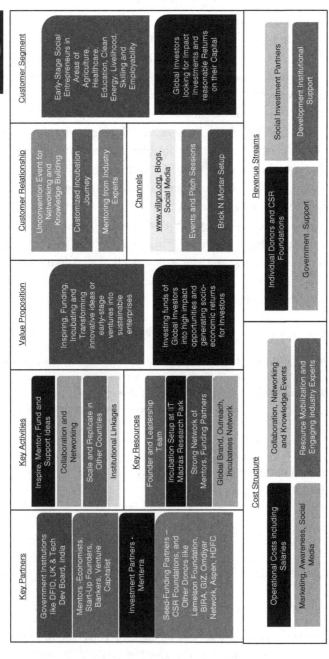

Figure 5 Villgro – Business model overview

Source: Authors' creation – Villgro Website (2019); VIR (2018); Analysis done by authors in Business Model Template introduced by Osterwalder and Pigneur (2010)

farmers in converting their ideas into businesses (Meghani, Jan 2018). Vineet scouted for innovative ideas that could help farmers improve efficiencies and converted those ideas into businesses. During his stint with GIAN, Vineet learned that nurturing an innovation into a sustainable and high-impact business, especially at the grassroots level, requires entrepreneurs and not innovators in the lead role. Entrepreneurs need access to risk capital and systemic mentoring for transforming an innovative idea into a viable and high-impact business model. This thinking led Vineet to go out on his own and set up Aavishkaar in 2001. Aavishkaar means "invention" in Hindi. Since its inception, Aavishkaar has been driven by a vision to catalyze development in underserved regions of India and other developing countries. This involves identifying entrepreneurs with high-impact ideas and providing them with risk capital and a nurturing environment thereby building sustainable enterprises having direct and indirect social impact on the millions of poor. It took Vineet five years to raise INR 50 million for Aavishkaar's first fund launched in 2001 (Sarkar, Apr 2018). Since then, Aavishkaar has raised more than USD 300 million across six funds during 2001–2018.

Understanding the Socioeconomic Impact

During 2001–2018, Aavishkaar had an active portfolio of sixty-three equity investments in high-impact businesses, asset under management (AUM) worth USD 300 million and six funds in operation (Aavishkaar Website, 2019; AIR, 2018). The majority of the investments are in social businesses within low-income states (LIS) in India, followed by entry in four other developing nations, mainly in Asia. Aavishkaar has invested in social businesses focusing on the underserved needs in eight sectors, namely agriculture; education; healthcare; energy; supply chain; technology for development; water, sanitation, and waste management; and financial inclusion and micro-finance. As of 2018, Aavishkaar has generated reasonable social and economic returns for the investors from twenty-seven social businesses. The list keeps growing with every year thereby reflecting the effectiveness of Aavishkaar's impact investing business model. All these efforts and impact orientation have resulted in generation of more than 39,000 jobs at the BoP, more than 268,000 direct livelihood opportunities, 10.3 million indirect livelihood opportunities, formal market access towards basic needs for 84 million people at the BoP, 1.3 million MT CO_2 reduction, and 23,209 MT of waste recycling (AIR, 2018). As a next step, Aavishkaar has expanded beyond India and replicated the early-stage investing model into four other countries namely Indonesia, Pakistan, Bangladesh, and Sri Lanka.

How Does It Operate?

Aavishkaar is driven by the belief that an enterprise-based development approach can enhance livelihoods, reduce vulnerabilities, and bring about a systemic change in the lives of individuals in the low-income population (AIR, 2018). The company evaluates, invests in, and mentors those social businesses that gainfully engage rural and low-income individuals across the value chain as producers, users, employees, or owners to deliver socioeconomic returns. Aavishkaar Groups' financial ecosystem includes platforms – namely **Aavishkaar, IntelleGrow, Arohan, and Tribe3** – for equity funding, venture debt funding, microfinancing, and advisory services for high-impact growth enterprises. Aavishkaar invests equity capital in high-risk and high-impact businesses in the ticket range of USD 500 k to USD 10 million. IntelleGrow funds underbanked, high-impact yet smaller enterprises with capital outlay in the range of USD 75 k to USD 1.5 million. Arohan addresses the financial needs of micro-enterprises run by low-income individuals with micro-finance loans in the range of USD 150 to USD 1,500. Finally, Tribe3 has been set up as a digital lending platform that empowers small business owners with quick and easy access to debt financing.

The company follows a three-step strategy to create a win-win ecosystem for the investors, investees, the BoP segment, and itself. The first step involves identifying and supporting high-impact social entrepreneurs through provision of capital and expert business inputs at various stages of growth via a sow, tend, and reap strategy.

The second step involves building an impact-oriented entrepreneurial ecosystem to showcase the power of incubation in nurturing high-impact social enterprises across developing economies, thereby increasing the availability and flow of investments in these kinds of high-impact initiatives. The third step involves undertaking responsible exits at an appropriate time from highly scalable and impactful businesses thereby generating commercial returns for the investors.

Aavishkaar is credited with three key innovations in venture capital investing in India. The first innovation involves shifting the investment risk from product or technology innovation to innovation in execution. This has led to core focus on the needs of the people and has resulted in a higher success ratio at the enterprise level despite geographical dispersion of enterprises in less-developed regions of India. The second innovation involves redefining the metrics of successful investment from economic returns of 100X to 3X–5X times. The third innovation involves engaging young, experienced, and passionate investment managers as employees who are driven by social recognition and fulfillment at work. The hard work, commitment, and passion of employees has been a major factor in Aavishkaar's success. This has enabled Aavishkaar to build a high-impact, passionate team with limited fees and no grant support. Regarding agriculture and food processing, the company has invested in solutions like sustainable fishing and fish processing; setting up alternate raw-material supply chains and engagement of farmers; near-to-farm crop storage and warehousing solutions; maximizing productivity of farmers and enhancing demand for highly nutritious crops; improving the procurement value chain, etc. Regarding the supply chain, Aavishkaar's investments include enterprises involved in setting up backend and frontend supply chains to the last-mile; an omni-channel platform for rural artisans; and fair trade and sustainable solutions for better products and incomes at the BoP. In education, Aavishkaar has invested in solutions related to delivery of better content and formal education via technology across the schools in India. Regarding healthcare, the company has invested in solutions linked to delivery of affordable, primary and secondary healthcare solutions in tier-II and tier-III cities and villages across India. Similarly, water, sanitation, and waste management solutions backed by Aavishkaar include delivery of clean drinking water across villages via community-centric water purification systems; setting up waste management systems with backend linkages and income opportunities for the low-income segment; as well as nontraditional and portable sanitation solutions. Energy, financial, and technology development solutions backed by Aavishkaar include backend supply networks for procurement and delivery of biomass to third-party power generation companies; fuel efficiency and cost optimization; technology-led power generation based upon renewable sources like micro hydel or biomass; technology-driven setup for last-mile logistics delivery; technology channel for skilling the workforce; and technology solutions for enabling access to formal and low-cost financing.

Vineet Rai and his company are driven by the philosophy of extraordinary risk-taking, tightly managed expansion, and looking out for opportunities in distressed locations (Meghani, Jan 2018). This philosophy made Aavishkaar proceed with an investment in Milk Mantra in 2011. At that time, the Odisha-based dairy company existed as a business plan on paper. The tiling of land and animal husbandry were not commonplace in that region during that time. Moreover, the organized channel for milk procurement in Eastern India was a mere 10 percent, as compared to national average of 23 percent. However, Vineet Rai observed a significant opportunity here, knowing that Odisha had many famous cities and a high demand for packaged milk (Meghani, Jan 2018). So, he went ahead with an investment into Milk Mantra's **"ethical sourcing"** model and guided Milk Mantra in the end-to-end set up of a local supply chain, thereby creating livelihood opportunities for thousands of people in the region. Figure 6 provides a detailed overview regarding Aavishkaar's business model.

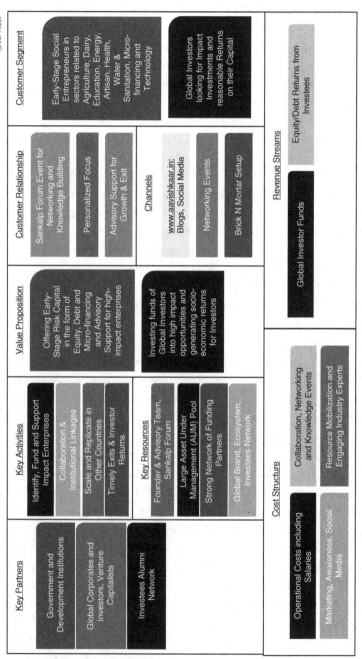

Figure 6 Aavishkaar – Business model overview

Source: Authors' creation – Aavishkaar Website (2019); AIR (2018); Analysis done by authors in Business Model Template introduced by Osterwalder and Pigneur (2010)

4.3 Rang De

Our mission is to make poverty history in India by addressing credit needs of underserved communities here ... We strive to achieve this through a network of individuals and social investors spread across the country.
— Smita Ramakrishna, Cofounder, Rang De (Thomas, Sep 2018)

Mission

To enable Indians to invest in and support the entrepreneurial and educational needs of low-income households. This involves connecting individual social investors to the community of curated entrepreneurs and students from across the country.

What Is the Underlying Context and Background?

Financial inclusion plays a very important role in bringing people above the poverty line or preventing people from moving below the poverty line. However, a significant proportion of the BoP population in India lacks access to the formal market ecosystem for getting low-cost loans from banking institutions in India. This segment is poor and lacks a banking credit history and is unable to commit any collateral against loans. Financial exclusion forces the BoP segment to take micro-credit at exorbitant interest rates from local moneylenders, resulting in getting trapped into financial exploitation and perennial cycles of debt, poverty, and suicides.

Micro-credit came up as an alternative to banking loans and exploitation by moneylenders. This involves setting up an ecosystem for disbursing small-size loans that are collateral free, and are lent to low-income households to meet their working capital/consumption needs. Typically, the loan size varies from INR 1,000 to INR 50,000. These loans are usually utilized for income-generation activities. The investee then repays the loans according to a preset repayment plan.

Rang De got started in 2008 with the simple idea of promoting financial inclusion at the BoP in India by bringing together individual social investors and low-income micro-entrepreneurs looking for low-cost and short-term micro-credit (Rang De Website, 2019).

Rang De decided to adopt a different business model from traditional micro-financing institutions. It set up a social peer-to-peer (P2P) crowdfunding or fundraising platform. At one end, this P2P platform has enabled access to low-cost funds for low-income individuals or investees at 16–18 APR (annual percentage rate). At other end, the P2P platform has enabled investors to make a choice of investees.

According to the founders' beliefs, timely and low-cost financial inclusion has a three-pronged impact on low-income communities – community, family, and individual. At the **community level**, it sets off a chain reaction of positive development within small communities. This helps the micro-enterprises to sustain and grow, thereby opening up multiple employment opportunities in rural India. At the **family level**, timely access to low-cost credit results in sustainable income generation and access to better healthcare, education, and other basic needs. At the **individual level**, financial inclusion with access to low-cost credit develops confidence and financial discipline among investees at the BoP resulting in focused and sustainable livelihood projects (Rang De Website, 2019).

Understanding the Socioeconomic Impact

Since its inception in 2008, Rang De has come a long way in terms of impact and outreach. The company enjoys a high repayment rate of 93 percent despite lending to high-risk individuals without financial backup or security. As of 2019, Rang De's P2P crowdfunding platform has created an active community of 15,000 social investors and has disbursed more than 60,000 loans (Thomas, Sep 2018). It has developed a network of more than sixteen impact partners across states like Manipur, Odisha, Maharashtra, and Madhya Pradesh. There are more than 60,000 female investees or borrowers who gained access to low-cost micro-credit from the Rang De platform. The company has disbursed more than INR 800 million to underserved communities for their livelihood, education, and healthcare needs across eighteen states in India (Rang De Website, 2019).

How Does It Operate?

Rang De (www.rangde.org) became registered as a charitable trust in 2018. To comply with the latest Reserve Bank of India (RBI) guidelines restricting peer-to-peer lending only to nonbanking financial companies (NBFCs), Rang De (www.rangde.in) has been registered as a for-profit NBFC P2P entity (Rang De Website, 2019).

Rang De prefers to continue as more of a social business rather than as a for-profit or not-for-profit entity. Social business implies that Rang De wants to maintain a culture of accountability and rigor similar to for-profits, and a commitment to the cause inherent in NGOs (**ET, Jan 2014**). Rang De believes in the philosophy of changing the way it sees change happen. The company is driven by a belief in empathy, not sympathy; a helping hand, not a handout; and power, not promises. The key differentiator in the business model of Rang De vis-à-vis other traditional micro-financing institutions (MFIs) is the crowdfunding approach wherein it raises the funds at lower interest rates from thousands of individual social investors rather than relying on banking institutions for raising the funds at higher interest rates. This enables Rang De to support the investees with far lower lending rates as compared to traditional MFIs. The whole idea behind the success of Rang De lies in strengthening the trust and transparency between the investor and investee. Rang De ensures the same by focusing on four key aspects: expanding grassroots partnerships, curating, ensuring transparency, and security. Grassroots partnerships involve developing a strong network of credible impact partner organizations who can authenticate the investees, deliver the funds, track the progress, and collect the paybacks, etc. Curating implies identifying low-income individuals and groups who need urgent funding for livelihood, education, or healthcare-related needs, lack access to credit from banks, and will pay back the loan in a timely way. Ensuring transparency means a commitment that 100 percent of the capital invested by social investors will go to their choice of investees and regular updates will be provided on the value addition and paybacks. Security means maintaining the confidentiality, integrity, and security of the personal details of the social investors.

> Interest rates that a borrower pays for the loan product is published on the website. We also provide regular updates to our social investors and routinely hold offline meetings in different cities where all players – from social investors to borrowers – get together.
> **– Smita Ramakrishna, Cofounder, Rang De** (Thomas,
> Sep 2018)

The operational model works as follows. Rang De receives a loan application from an investee like a micro-entrepreneur or student, screens the loan request, and if convinced, launches the loan/funding story on its P2P portal with a due date. The social investor (SI) chooses a micro-entrepreneur or student he/she would like to support through the Rang De website. SI makes an investment of any amount above INR 100 in the investee's loan. Once the loan is fully funded, funds are transferred into the investee's bank account. In case the loan is not fully funded by the due date, it is cancelled and the invested amount is returned to the Rang De credit account of the respective investors. The investee pays back the loan as per the repayment schedule at an agreed upon interest rate. Rang De's mission is to ensure that investees pay an affordable interest rate on their loans. The loan products are customized as per the individual investee's need. The highest interest rate that an investee will pay for a loan through Rang De is 10 percent flat per annum, which is equivalent to 18 percent APR. This interest amount gets split between the social investor, Rang De, and impact partners. Around 50 percent of the interest amount goes to the impact partners and the remaining 50 percent gets split between the social investor and Rang De. The social investor gets a corresponding amount in the form of Rang De credit along with a nominal interest rate equivalent to savings interest in a bank. Rang De credit can be used to fund other investees or can be withdrawn from Rang De by the investor. Rang De's network of impact partners plays a significant role in ensuring the transparency of the complete cycle from funding to paybacks. Impact partners are responsible for identifying real needs, authenticating entrepreneur and student profiles, and facilitating disbursal and recovery of loans. Impact partners are also responsible for conducting financial literacy trainings, and mentoring individual investees in financial discipline in terms of cash-flow management, building a positive credit history, and timely paybacks.

Timely access to fair micro-credit leads to financial independence for low-income households. For example, a differently abled woman runs a grocery shop in a poor community. She took over the grocery store when her father passed away. While running the store, she realized that expanding the number of items sold in the store would increase her clientele and earnings. She required short-term funds for expansion but was unable to get the same from banking institutions. She applied to Rang De for micro-credit. She received the micro-credit and that increased her monthly earnings to more than INR 7,000 per month. This increase in income helped her to save more and take care of her elderly mother (Rang De Website, 2019). Figure 7 provides a detailed overview regarding Rang De's business model.

4.4 Phool (Help Us Green)

I am impressed by your Phool enterprise in India which is perfect example of circular economy. Keep setting the standards for others to follow.
– Paul Polman, CEO, Unilever, 5th March 2017 (Phool Website, 2019)

Mission

To preserve the Ganges river and empower women of marginalized communities by providing them a means to earn their livelihood.

What Is the Underlying Context and Background?

The genesis of "Phool," a social business, lies in two societal and environmental anomalies. First, there are over 200 million "Dalits," also known as untouchables, in India. The majority of these people live and transact in an informal economy. There is a lack of social acceptance, especially for the lower caste sanitation workers, who lie at the bottom of hierarchical caste system and are mainly involved in cleaning up the sewers and human waste. These people face social and economic discrimination as well as domestic violence. Second,

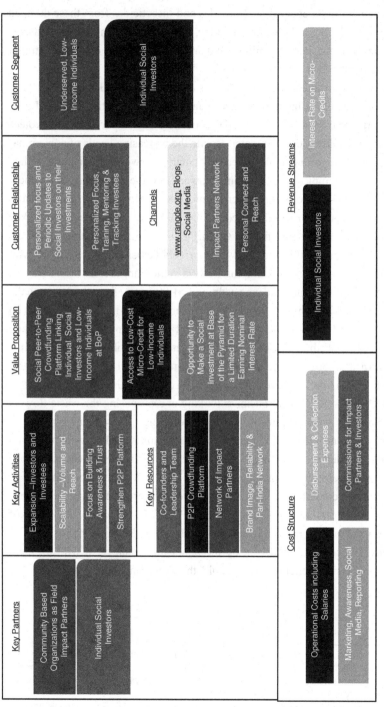

Figure 7 Rang De – Business model overview

Source: Authors' creation – Rang De Website (2019); Analysis done by authors in Business Model Template introduced by Osterwalder and Pigneur (2010)

around 8 million tons of waste flowers are getting dumped into holy rivers like the Ganges in India every day. Pesticides and insecticides from these dumped flowers get mixed into holy water making it highly toxic. The Ganges water is a lifeline for more than 400 million Indians and is used for drinking, bathing, farming, fishing, etc.

The idea regarding recycling of flowers dumped into the Ganges river by the places of worship in India was born in January 2015. On the day of **Makar Sankranti,**[5] two friends visited the banks of the Ganges river and saw devotees drinking and bottling up river water despite the increasing levels of contamination due to waste effluents from nearby tanneries, sewers, and factories. They also saw how temples were dumping flowers into the Ganges river and how those flowers were also being converted into muck when mixed with other water pollutants. This observation stayed in the minds of both friends and they decided to explore this a bit further. On further research, they found that flowers being offered and getting dumped in the rivers across India are loaded with pesticides and insecticides. Dumping flowers in the Ganges river means mixing toxic chemicals (arsenic, lead, and cadmium >1,000 ppm) from flowers with the river water making it highly toxic (PH[6] 4.7) and resulting in adverse impacts on marine life and people. Around 86.5 percent of child mortality in India and Bangladesh is attributed to toxic drinking-water issues like cholera, hepatitis, and diarrhea (Phool Website, 2019; Chakraborty, Feb 2018).

In May 2015, this realization led to the birth of **"Help Us Green,"** also called **"Phool,"** a for-profit social business looking at repurposing the waste flowers from places of worship into organic value offerings. Both friends spent significant time and effort on experimentation, creating market awareness, and pitching the idea of managing flower waste from religious places to various stakeholders before gaining acceptance and belief. After eighteen months of efforts, they were able to conceive of recycled-flower incense and vermicompost as value offerings. During 2015–19, "Phool" has expanded the range of organic value offerings by diversifying into biodegradable packaging and bio-leathers. The company is driven by the belief that whatever it will do, there should be a visible benefit for the people, the community, and the Ganges.

---

[5] Makar Sankranti is a festival dedicated to SUN deity. This day is celebrated on January 14 or 15 of every year. On this day, people celebrate the solar cycle thereby marking the end of the month with the winter solstice and the start of longer days. https://mythgyaan.com/makar-sankranti-pongal-uttarayan-2018/ (last accessed 22 Sep 2019).

[6] PH (potential of hydrogen) refers to the hydrogen ion concentration in a solution. It measures the acidity or alkalinity of a solution. www.javatpoint.com/ph-full-form (last accessed 22 Sep 2019).

Understanding the Socioeconomic Impact

During 2015–2019, the company came a long way from identification of technology to female empowerment to cleaning up the Ganges river (Phadke, Dec 2018). Starting with an initial capital of INR 72,000 in 2015, the company has raised more than 1 million dollars to date (Phadke, Dec 2018). The company employs seventy-three women from marginalized communities full time. It has recycled more than 11,060 tons of flower waste and off-set 11 tons of pesticide from polluting the Ganges. The company collects more than 8.4 tons of flower waste from temples of Uttar Pradesh in India on a daily basis and handcrafts those flowers into charcoal-free incense, vermicompost, and biodegradable packaging material using **"flowercycling"** technology. The company aims to expand the production scale and capacity by setting up manufacturing plants across multiple locations in India. By 2020, it aims to recycle 50 tons of waste flowers daily, and to hire more than 3,500 women. It is also working with the Uttar Pradesh Government to form the first policy around temple waste management (Phadke, Dec 2018).

How Does It Operate?

Phool's (www.phool.co) business model is driven by three questions. Why should sacred flowers pollute the rivers? Why should low-caste and low-income women be denied access to opportunity? Why should anyone bear the illeffects of toxic chemicals?

The company has a long history of research and hard work. Before beginning operations, the founders spoke to multiple botany professors, farmers, vermicomposting experts, temple heads, and flower traders to learn about the best alternatives for recycling the waste flowers. They tested composting waste flowers with different types of dung (cow, sheep, goat, horse, etc.) and combinations to find out the best NPK (nitrogen-phosphorus-potassium) value of vermicompost (Sinigdha, Jan 2016). The ongoing research efforts of six months led to the development of a mineral- and enzyme-rich recipe having seventeen natural ingredients, labelled as **"Mitti."** This combination is a safer and smarter alternative to chemical fertilizers with zero carbon footprint. **"Mitti"** involves coffee residue as one of the ingredients, resulting in a significant boost to the nitrogen content. The company partnered with coffee shops in Kanpur for collecting coffee residue (Sinigdha, Jan 2016).

Once the company finalized the scope and approach for recycling flower waste, it decided to engage low-income women in the value chain. The details of the day-to-day operational value chain are as follows. The first step involves collecting flower waste from temples and bringing the same to the manufacturing facility on a daily basis. Second, flowers are segregated by hand, which involves separating out plastic, paper, etc. from the flowers. Third, organic bioculum[7] is sprayed on the segregated flower waste to offset the chemical residue. Fourth, flowers are washed thoroughly and water used for washing is collected and used in vermicomposting. Fifth, flowers petals are separated and dried in the sun. Sixth, depending upon the flower types and carotenoid levels, the dried flowers are used for organic incense sticks or vermicomposting or producing florafoam, a biodegradable packaging material.

Regarding incense sticks, dried petals are powdered and mixed with natural plants resins along with in-house ingredients to make a dough. The dough is hand-rolled using an innovative method to make raw incense sticks and cones. The hand-rolling method has been adopted to ensure chemical-free incense sticks as opposed to the traditional method that involves carcinogenic coal for making incense sticks. Dried incense sticks and cones are then dipped into essential oils and packed into incense boxes. While doing the packaging, the company has implemented another innovative idea. The company observed that people tend to resist disposing of packing boxes or materials having a photo of God into dustbins. For anything with packaging material having image of God, the company uses seed paper. In this packaging, seeds are fused into the paper material and when this packing material is planted in a pot, a plant sprouts, thereby preserving the respect for God figures (**Sinigdha, Jan 2016**).

> *The only non-degradable part of our product was the packaging. We fused paper cellulose with cellulose from seeds for the packaging and after you use the product, you can plant the wrapper in a pot. – **Ankit Agarwal, Founder, Phool** (Kondepudy, July 2016)*

Further, incense packaging boxes also carry a colorful photo of the female employees. This brings a sense of pride and recognition among the employees.

> *It's such a nice idea to have our photo in the box – whoever buys this will know I have packed it. My kids and family even tease me saying I am now known all over India! I am so happy doing this." – **Sujatha, Women Employee at Phool** (Phadke, Dec 2018)*

Regarding vermicomposting, the green parts of the dried flowers and leaves are mixed with cow dung, seventeen different elements, and in-house ingredients. Earthworms are added to eat up the waste and make vermicompost.

---

[7] Bioculum is environment-friendly facilitator for aerobic composting of organic waste. www.youtube.com/watch?v=mQMKmUkLbY8 (last accessed 22 Sep 2019).

Regarding florafoam, dried petals are molded with natural fungi to make biodegradable packaging material.

The most important aspect of this value chain is that all the work is done by women, who were earlier marginalized due to their prior engagement with sanitation work. A work opportunity with "Phool" has resulted in a socioeconomic transformation for these women in terms of better income, good work–life balance, access to education for their children, and social acceptance. All women employees at "Phool" get health, insurance, and retirement benefits, access to clean drinking water, and access to other facilities at par with anybody else. This has made a big change in the psyche and confidence of these women.

The company ensures that the end products are fully organic and chemical free. To ensure organic value offerings, the company invests significant time, capital, and effort in Research and Development (R&D) and innovation. The company has set up a team of seven research scientists in the R&D lab at IIT, Kanpur incubation center (Phadke, Dec 2018). Figure 8 provides a detailed overview regarding Phool's business model.

4.5 NEPRA Resource Management Pvt. Ltd. (Let's Recycle)

There is pressure now on the whole ecosystem to manage air, water and solid waste. Companies, too, have high sustainability parameters. The opportunity is going to be crazy over the coming months.

    – Sandeep Patel, CEO, NEPRA (Nair-Ghaswalla, May 2019)

Our aim is to establish Let's Recycle – NEPRA as the leader and the go-to company for large-scale dry waste management. We have seen impressive growth in Ahmedabad and this new round of funding from Aavishkaar and Asha Impact will help us expand our operations to three more cities and help us build the foundation for expansion across the country over the next five years.

    – Sandeep Patel, CEO, NEPRA (MCN, Jul 2018)

Guiding Principle

Creating equality and respect for a welcoming workplace, intending to create social and economic inclusion through operations, and creating a broader impact for the society and environment (NEPRA Website, 2019).

What Is the Underlying Context and Background?

India is facing a huge waste-management challenge with increasing urbanization. Around 377 million people living in urban India generate more than 62 million MT of municipal solid waste (MSW) per annum (Lahiry,

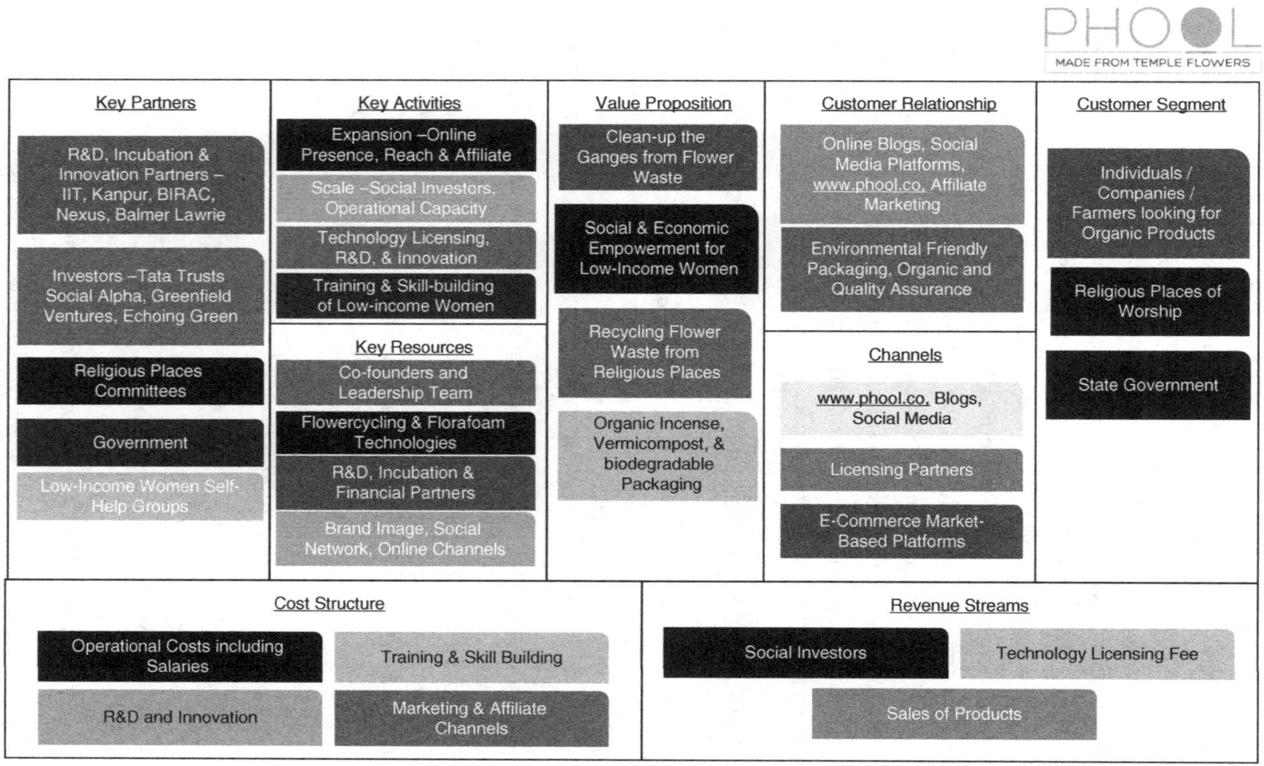

PHOOL
MADE FROM TEMPLE FLOWERS

Key Partners

R&D, Incubation & Innovation Partners – IIT, Kanpur, BIRAC, Nexus, Balmer Lawrie

Investors – Tata Trusts Social Alpha, Greenfield Ventures, Echoing Green

Religious Places Committees

Government

Low-income Women Self-Help Groups

Key Activities

Expansion – Online Presence, Reach & Affiliate

Scale – Social investors, Operational Capacity

Technology Licensing, R&D, & innovation

Training & Skill-building of Low-income Women

Key Resources

Co-founders and Leadership Team

Flowercycling & Florafoam Technologies

R&D, Incubation & Financial Partners

Brand Image, Social Network, Online Channels

Value Proposition

Clean-up the Ganges from Flower Waste

Social & Economic Empowerment for Low-income Women

Recycling Flower Waste from Religious Places

Organic Incense, Vermicompost, & biodegradable Packaging

Customer Relationship

Online Blogs, Social Media Platforms, www.phool.co, Affiliate Marketing

Environmental Friendly Packaging, Organic and Quality Assurance

Channels

www.phool.co, Blogs, Social Media

Licensing Partners

E-Commerce Market-Based Platforms

Customer Segment

Individuals / Companies / Farmers looking for Organic Products

Religious Places of Worship

State Government

Cost Structure

Operational Costs including Salaries

R&D and Innovation

Training & Skill Building

Marketing & Affiliate Channels

Revenue Streams

Social Investors

Technology Licensing Fee

Sales of Products

Figure 8 Phool – Business model overview

Source: Authors' creation – Phool Website (2019); Analysis done by authors in Business Model Template introduced by Osterwalder and Pigneur (2010)

May 2019; IWP 2019). This is equivalent to around 0.8 kilograms of solid waste generated per person per day. MSW contains around 51 percent organic waste, 17 percent recyclables, 11 percent hazardous, and 21 percent inert waste. Around 60 percent of the generated MSW gets collected (Lahiry, May 2019; IWP 2019). However, only one-third of the collected waste gets treated and remaining two-thirds gets dumped in landfill sites. The majority of waste management companies follow a **"lifting and shifting"** model. This involves merely transporting the solid waste from waste generation sites to landfills in exchange for tipping fees paid by the municipalities (Empea, Oct 2018). This has led to increasing numbers of landfill sites appearing across cities in India, a kind of solid-waste dump yard having significant health hazards for the human beings and animals. Whatever does not get collected, remains segregated on the streets and poses health, sanitation, and environmental problems. MSW generation in India is expected to increase by more than two times to around 137 million MT by 2025 (Empea, Oct 2018).

One point of note is that a significant amount of MSW collection is being done by individual waste pickers. There are around three million waste pickers in India and the majority of these pickers are poor women and children (Dandapani, Nov 2017). These waste pickers do the pick-up, cleaning, sorting, and segregation of solid waste before selling the same to scrap dealers for day-to -day living. Waste pickers start their day early in the morning; walk for 8–10 kilometers to mutually agreed-upon locations; scavenge in dump sites, streets, and alleyways; bend a minimum of 1,000 times; collect around 20 kilograms of recyclable waste with bare hands; and sort and sell the same for a meagre income of INR 100–150 per day (Tiwari, Jun 2018; Dandapani, Nov 2017). The same cycle continues every day leading to health hazards for these waste pickers, the majority of whom are illiterate, unskilled, and migrants having no permanent residence. These people do not get societal recognition and lack access to various social welfare schemes offered by the government.

Sandeep Patel, Dhrumin Patel, and Ravi Patel identified this socioeconomic and environmental gap as an opportunity. In 2011, this led to the set up of NEPRA Resource Management Pvt. Ltd. as a solid waste recycling company in India. NEPRA's Let's Recycle initiative focuses on providing sustainable solid waste collection and recycling solutions for communities and organizations across India.

Understanding the Socioeconomic Impact

NEPRA's Let's Recycle initiative has created significant socioeconomic and environmental impact during 2012–2018.

From an environmental perspective, the company has facilitated more than 500 organizations in their go-green and recycling efforts. NEPRA's Enterprise Resource Planning (ERP)-driven waste management solution has facilitated recycling of more than 880 MT of paper, 5,107 MT of plastic, and more than 2,000 MT of glass. During 2012–16, the company diverted 10,616 MT waste from landfills resulting in savings of 3,159 MT carbon-dioxide (CO_2) equivalent emissions. All these initiatives and efforts have resulted in savings of more than 14,995 trees, 1.76 million liters of water, 32.12 million Kilowatt-hour (kWh) of energy, and 13.61 million liters of oil (NEPRA Website, 2019). The company has the capacity to process more than 100 MT of waste every day (Rai, Jun 2018). The company has collected and recycled more than 27,000 MT of solid waste to date and planned to divert more than 30,000 MT of waste from landfills by 2020 (Dandapani, Nov 2017).

From a social perspective, Let's Recycle has formalized India's unorganized and unregulated waste management sector by setting up an integrated, transparent, and fair-price ecosystem for marginalized waste collectors. The company has integrated more than 1,800 waste pickers into the formal economy and provides them fair prices, transparent services, and immediate cash payments directly without any intermediary. NEPRA's efforts towards setting up an organized waste collection ecosystem and eliminating the intermediaries has led to an increase in income of waste pickers by 30–40 percent, besides getting other benefits like health insurance, identification card, and opportunities for the education of children (Dandapani, Nov 2017).

How Does It Operate?

NEPRA has built a supply chain that connects dry-waste generators and collectors to recyclers thereby integrating more than 1,800 waste collectors in the formal economy (Rai, Jun 2018). The company undertakes the collection and sorting, and facilitates recycling of a range of solid waste material including commercial and industrial waste, paper and cardboard, metal, glass, plastic, and wood (NEPRA Website, 2019). Let's Recycle signs up different types of companies and associations as customers and develops a customized waste management plan, tailored and scheduled for them, depending upon their requirements. The company offers single-stream recycling services to the clients. This enables customers ease of placing all acceptable recyclable materials into a single bin. For waste collection and disposal, the company has set up an integrated fleet management system. This includes a route management software, known as General Packet Radio Service (GPRS), and ERP software setup. The technology ecosystem ensures the shortest route for waste collection and disposal, thereby ensuring significant cost savings, time reduction, and decrease in CO_2 emissions. ERP system enables near real-time tracking of waste pick-up, handling, and reporting activities so as to make the system more authentic and efficient.

During 2011–2019, NEPRA's Let's Recycle initiative went through significant changes in terms of value chain, process innovations, and business model transformation. Aavishkaar, an impact investor, has played a significant role in the transformation. Before Aavishkaar's involvement, NEPRA's Material Recovery Facility (MRF), where recyclable materials are received, segregated, and sorted, was rudimentary and unorganized. Manual segregation and sorting of MSW used to result in operational inefficiencies and suboptimal operating conditions for the waste pickers. Mentoring from Aavishkaar resulted in mechanization of MRF and the addition of essential processes like grinding and washing of plastic waste. Due to this, inventory levels got reduced from fifty days in 2013 to two days in 2018. The productivity of workers improved from segregation of 50 kilograms to 300 kilograms of solid waste per day (Dandapani, Nov 2017). NEPRA set up an advanced management information system (MIS) and fleet tracking software. Use of vehicle tracking software and optimized route planning led to the decrease in waste collection costs by more than 33 percent between 2013 and 2018 (Dandapani, Nov 2017).

Around 10–15 percent of the overall waste collection in India involves mixing of wet kitchen waste resulting in mixed waste. It is always difficult to segregate wet waste from solid waste. The same challenge was faced by NEPRA. Until 2016, it used to aggregate the mixed waste and dump it into a landfill site. In 2016, NEPRA developed a use case for this mixed waste as refuse-derived fuel[8] (RDF) and started selling this to cement companies as an alternative to fossil fuels in their cement kilns. As a result, NEPRA is positioned today as a **"zero waste to landfill"** company (Dandapani, Nov 2017).

NEPRA's business model has made a significant impact in the lives of more than 1,800 waste pickers who are engaged with the company. As the company's operations have grown, it employs more than 250 full-time people from low-income socioeconomic backgrounds. It offers them health and safety training as well as retirement benefits, access to banking, and health insurance. Figure 9 provides a detailed overview regarding NEPRA's business model.

---

[8] RDF is the product of processing MSW to separate the non-combustible from the combustible portion and preparing the combustible portion into a form that can be effectively used as an alternate fuel in cement and other industries. waste.zendesk.com/hc/en-us/articles/212349717-What-is-Refuse-Derived-Fuel-RDF-; http://cpheeo.gov.in/upload/5bda791e5afb3SBMRDFBook.pdf (last accessed 29 Sep 2019).

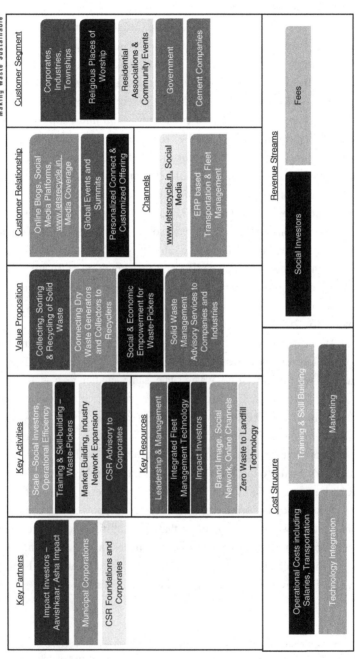

Figure 9 NEPRA – Let's Recycle – Business model overview

Source: Authors' creation – NEPRA Website (2019); Nair-Ghaswalla, A. (May 2019); Rai (Jun 2018); Empea (Oct 2018); Analysis done by authors in Business Model Template introduced by Osterwalder and Pigneur (2010)

4.6 Piramal Sarvajal

Problems of poverty are, on most occasions, inextricably linked with those of water – its availability, its proximity, its quantity, and its quality.

(UN World Water Report, 2015)

The Soochak makes it so easy to operate the machine. It is simple to maintain it and also to contact the company. It keeps the machine in good condition and allows me to use it properly but it also attracts a lot of customers.

*– **Jitenbhai, Franchisee** (Sarvajal Website, 2019)*

The variety of issues is so huge in the social space, that you need at least 5–10 pilot projects before people come on board. Thinking that I will just start one thing, stick to it and solve the problems does not happen. By very nature of a social enterprise, low cost and high-quality solutions are needed and it will need trying out different concepts.

– Anuj Sharma, CEO, Piramal Sarvajal (Punia, July 2013)

Mission

To innovate, demonstrate, enable, and promote affordable, safe, drinking water solutions (Sarvajal Website, 2019).

What is the Underlying Context and Background?

There are around 170 million people in India who lack access to clean drinking water (Samhita, 20XX). More than two-thirds of India relies on groundwater for drinking water requirements. Unfortunately, nearly 75 percent of the surface water is contaminated with arsenic and fluoride (Samhita, 20XX). Nearly 0.5 million children succumb to preventable water-borne diseases like cholera and diarrhea every year in India. Nearly 21 percent of the health issues reported in India are due to contaminated drinking water (DG, March 2019). This has created a major cost overhead for the low-income families who end up spending a significant proportion of their annual income on water-borne health issues (Sarvajal Website, 2019; Samhita, 20XX). India loses more than 73 million working days and 443 million school days annually due to water-borne diseases (DG, March 2019). More than 66 million people in 20 states of India are at risk due to excessive fluoride content in water. Another 10 million people face health risks due to excessive arsenic content in drinking water (DG, March 2019). Around 6 million children below 14 years of age suffer from fluorosis-related health issues (DG, March 2019). The majority of states in India are getting into a water crisis situation with the rapid depletion of ground water. As per the current situation in 2019, more than 25 million people lack access to safe drinking water in India. There are more than 1,600 deaths daily due to acute diarrhea. Rural women waste more than 700 hours per annum in travelling long distances for getting drinking water (Sarvajal Website, 2019; Samhita, 20XX). Water-related diseases lead to multiple health issues, which in turn results in more than INR 360 million lost for the economy annually (Sarvajal Website, 2019).

Piramal's hometown, Bagar in water-scarce region of Rajasthan, faced a similar situation (Sarvajal Website, 2019; Samhita, 20XX). Piramal Foundation started a pilot project, which involved eliminating fluoride contamination in drinking water used by the people of Bagar. This pilot project led to several technology and business-process innovations. The success of the Bagar water initiative led to the genesis of Piramal Water Pvt. Ltd. in 2008, which is known as Sarvajal today (Sarvajal Website, 2019; Samhita, 20XX). Piramal Foundation set up Sarvajal, a mission-driven social enterprise in 2008 for providing community-level safe drinking water to the underserved population across water-scarce regions in India (Sarvajal Website, 2019). Sarvajal in Sanskrit means **"water for all."** These community-level solutions are locally operated but centrally managed on a market-based, pay-per-use system.

Understanding the Socioeconomic Impact

During 2008–19, Sarvajal came a long way in terms of scale, outreach, and socioeconomic impact. The company has set up more than 1,000 purification units and 575 solar-powered ATMs across India. More than 632,000 people from the low-income segment are now served clean drinking water on a daily basis across nineteen states in India (Sarvajal Website, 2019).

How Does It Operate?

When Sarvajal started in 2008, it observed that lack of awareness among the communities regarding water-borne health issues and associated medical costs was a major inhibitor in adoption of safe drinking water solutions offered by the company. The company set up a Community Awareness and Local Marketing (CALM) team to ensure last-mile connection, systemic communication, and awareness among people living in water-scarce regions. It engages local men and women from water-scarce communities, trains them, and leverages their community-level trust and relationship for creating awareness among the masses regarding water-borne diseases and the significance of clean drinking water. The CALM team manages day-to-day handholding of the franchisee, close interaction with customers and beneficiaries, as well as relationships with the key stakeholders on the field.

From a technological perspective, Sarvajal has pioneered the design, development, and deployment of remotely tracked community-level drinking water purification systems for the underserved population in remote locations across nineteen states in India (Sarvajal Website, 2019; Punia, July 2013). Use of technology has enabled operational efficiency, operator accountability, and better service for the communities. Sarvajal designs and manufactures technology agnostic, high-quality and low-cost water purification units, cloud-connected and solar-powered water ATMs, cloud-based monitoring systems for quality management, and also customized ERP to manage water purification projects (Punia, July 2013). The project is deployed and operated in collaboration with local entrepreneurs or local panchayat/CBOs. This has created sustainable livelihood opportunities for low-income micro-entrepreneurs. Sarvajal leases its water purification technology/equipment to a local entrepreneur who is identified as a franchisee owner. Sarvajal helps the franchisee in mobilizing funds from microlending institutions or project sponsors. Also, it provides training, payment solutions, customer service support, marketing material, and operational support and performance feedback to the franchise owners. Revenue gets shared between Sarvajal and the franchisees (Samhita, 20XX). For last-mile access and distribution, Sarvajal has set up solar-powered, cloud-operated water ATMs. Sarvajal has been granted two patents in the USA for the design of water ATMs (PS, March 2019). Water ATMs use smart cards for dispensing water to the customers. Use of smart cards ensures price transparency and quality assurance. Sarvajal offers two operating models to enable access to safe drinking water for the masses.

First model involves setting up a single unit community solution (Sarvajal Website, 2019). Every community gets a water treatment plan thereby eliminating any external dependency. This includes the following set of activities. A purification plant is installed in a community, like a village, school, etc. Water ATMs are installed within the community for ease of distribution, transparency, quality assurance, as well as tracking consumption patterns and consumer behavior. A local individual or entrepreneur is trained for managing the daily local operations and delivery channels. Customers can opt for home delivery, pick up from select local stores, or water ATMs or purification plants. The Sarvajal team ensures regular maintenance support, community awareness, and local marketing. Real-time data is collected from solar-powered and cloud-connected water ATMs and analyzed. Accordingly, daily and monthly performance reports are shared with the stakeholders.

Second model involves setting up a hub-and-spoke ecosystem (Sarvajal Website, 2019). Depending upon community-level demands, one or more communities share a water treatment plan for optimal utilization. This includes the following set of activities. A centrally located water purification plant or hub is set up having access to raw water and power. Water ATMs are installed in nearby communities and act as spokes. These water ATMs operate via solar power, are cloud-connected and can provide 24/7 access to safe drinking water. Filtered water is transferred from the purification system to water ATMs using hygienic water-carrying vehicles. The Sarvajal team ensures regular maintenance support, community awareness, and local marketing. Real-time data is collected from solar-powered and cloud-connected water ATMs and analyzed. Accordingly, daily and monthly performance reports are shared with the stakeholders.

Sarvajal's success is driven by the right mix of technology, innovation, and local engagement. The company pioneered last-mile operational accountability by making use of IoT for real-time monitoring and tracking of demand and supply. This also involves setting up water ATMs – solar-powered, cloud-connected and smart-card–based automatic water vending machines. Regarding the purification setup, Sarvajal uses five-step purification machines where each step can be customized as per local need and type of raw water availability. For example, fluoride content is high in North India. Due to open defecation in developing countries, pathogens like *Escherichia Coli* contaminate groundwater and infect people with water-borne diseases like cholera, typhoid, dysentery, etc. Water purification machines are equipped with remote monitoring and information layering. The company has developed a patented remote-monitoring device, "Soochak," which can be installed on a water purification plant. This device captures real-time data from the purification machines, which helps in getting insights into the social impact, outreach, and consumption patterns. Also, this device enables proactive maintenance and guides operators in the local language for any queries or issues. The company has implemented the Sarvajal enterprise management system (SEMS), an online platform for aggregating and analyzing real-time data from all water purification and dispensing units. Real-time data collection, analysis, and reporting enables deeper insights into consumer behavior, consumption patterns, operational efficiency, and socioeconomic returns on investments made by Sarvajal and corporate partners as a part of the CSR initiative. Figure 10 provides a detailed overview regarding Sarvajal's business model.

4.7 GARV Toilets

The need of the hour is to focus on self-sustainable, alternative public toilet models that can be replicated across geographies in an eco-friendly way.
– *Mayank Midha, Managing Partner, GARV Toilets* (GARV Website, 2019)

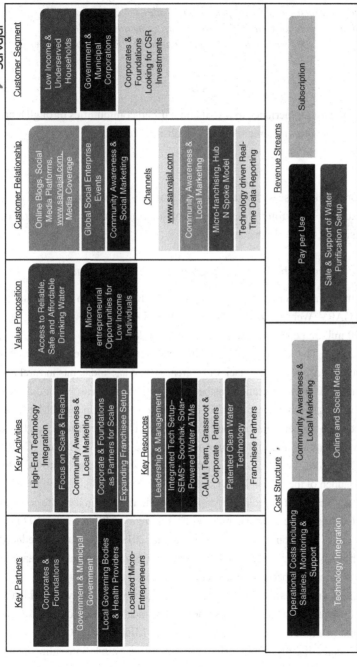

Figure 10 Piramal Sarvajal – Business model overview

*SEMS – Sarvajal Enterprise Management System. IoT and cloud-based real-time monitoring and support setup along with solar-powered water ATMs

Source: Authors' creation – Samhita (20XX); DG (March 2019); Sarvajal Website (2019); Analysis done by authors in Business Model Template introduced by Osterwalder and Pigneur (2010)

> *There is a real shortage of toilet infrastructure – and this crumbling infrastructure is bearing the load of ever-increasing migrant population from rural areas to urban areas. The government has relied on conventional brick-and-mortar structure toilet infrastructure for the past many decades, which has resulted in repeated failed implementations with billions of dollars going down the drain.*
> *– Mayank Midha, Managing Partner, GARV Toilets* (Idle, Jan 2019)

Vision

Providing rich user experience to low-income urban communities through tech-enabled smart sanitation centers (GARV Website, 2019).

Mission

To serve one million users daily through state-of-the-art, well-maintained toilet infrastructure by 2020 through integration of smart technology and generation of user insights (GARV Website, 2019).

What Is the Underlying Context and Background?

There are more than 2.3 billion people globally who lack access to basic sanitation facilities (GARV Website, 2019; Idle, Jan 2019). During 2015, there had been around 600 million people defecating in the open in India (GARV Website, 2019; Idle, Jan 2019). The key reasons that have contributed to these high numbers involve lack of access to toilets, lack of awareness, and age-old habits in rural and semi-urban India. Open defecation has been one of the major reasons for diarrheal diseases resulting in a high percentage of deaths among infants in India. Moreover, lack of access to proper sanitation and the practice of open defecation has led to a assault on the pride and dignity of women and the safety of children (GARV Website, 2019; Idle, Jan 2019). The open defecation situation has improved a lot due to the launch of the "Clean India Campaign" or "Swachh Bharat Abhiyaan" in 2014 by the government of India. According to World Bank estimates, the count of people defecating in the open has reduced from a high of 70 percent in 1990s to 45 percent in 2015 (Alexander & Padmanabhan, Mar 2019). This figure has reduced further during 2015–2019. However, there is still a lo"Swachh Bharat Abhiyaan"ng way to go before India becomes open-defecation free at the country level.

The **"Clean India Campaign"** acted as a starting point for Mayank Midha to develop a self-sustainable business model for tackling the social issue of hygiene and sanitation (Idle, Jan 2019). Mayank Midha set up GARV Toilets (**"GARV"** means dignity, honor, pride) in 2016 with the aim of providing a one-stop smart sanitation solution to the water, sanitation and hygiene (WASH) needs of the underserved communities in rural, semi-urban and urban areas

(GARV Website, 2019). While setting up GARV Toilets, Mayank and his team observed that the majority of public or community toilets in low-income areas are made up of traditional brick-n-mortar structures, face vandalism, and lack maintenance and basic necessities like water, electricity, and ventilation. All these issues make them dysfunctional and unusable within a short span of time. Whatever investment gets done into setting up these toilets, it goes to waste without any reasonable impact on the masses. This is a significant waste of CSR investments and government budget. Based upon trials, he decided to come up with a pre-fabricated public toilet having smart-technology features like RFID (Radio Frequency Identification) and IoT and basic convenience and maintainability attributes like solar power, LED (Light-Emitting Diode) lights, exhaust fan for ventilation, sanitary-pad vending machines, ramp access, hand rails for elderly and disabled people, overhead water tanks, a biodigester tank, bore wells, and a setup for wastewater recycling (GARV Website, 2019; Idle, Jan 2019). Using stainless steel for the pre-fabricated superstructure, toilet pans, and washbasins has proved to be a creative and cost-effective innovation as this had made the toilets vandal proof, easy to clean, and rust proof (Diervorst, Oct 2016). All the fittings in the toilets are either welded or fitted together with hidden nuts and bolts to prevent any vandalism (WNR, 2016). This means higher shelf life with lower operating costs (Diervorst, Oct 2016). Further, the use of a biodigester tank enables the company to set up toilets anywhere in the world, even at places that lack infrastructure to deal with wastewater (GARV Website, 2019; Idle, Jan 2019). Smart technology integration enables real-time updates to the monitoring agencies, government, and implementation partners in terms of usage pattern, hygiene behavior, and maintenance. Launch of smart sanitation solutions has led to a positive impact in the education of girl children as well as the restoration of pride, dignity, and safety of women.

Understanding the Socioeconomic Impact

During 2016–2019, GARV Toilets has made a significant contribution in terms of scale, reach, and socioeconomic impact. By 2019, the company had expanded its presence beyond India in Bhutan, Ghana, and Nigeria (GARV Website, 2019). The company has set up more than 700 toilets globally, offering around 0.3 million services on daily basis to the underserved segment (GARV Website, 2019). This has resulted in annual reduction of 102.4 MT of CO_2 emissions.

How Does It Operate?

GARV Toilets offers four distinctive categories of smart sanitation solutions. First solution involves setting up **"Peek-a-Poo"** toilets in schools (GARV Website, 2019). These are kid-friendly toilets for boys and girls. These are designed and implemented in diverse colors to attract the kids and develop basic hygiene habits among them from an early age. Second value offering is **"GARV Swabhimaan"** toilets for women. These toilets offer privacy, dignity, and pride to women and include sanitary-napkin vending machines and incinerators. Third value proposition involves **"GARV Galva" or "GARV Stainless Sparkle"** public or community toilets (GARV Website, 2019). These are galvanized or stainless steel toilets for underserved communities and incorporate smart technology setups. Fourth solution includes budget and environment-friendly steel toilets known as **"GARV Eco."** Another model offered by GARV toilets, which is primarily suitable for areas without sewerage connections, is the smart-toilet with biodigester tank (Diervorst, Oct 2016). A bio-digester tank processes the fecal matter through bacterial action, thereby eliminating the need for water supply during usage and maintenance. The only output is an odorless, colorless liquid that can be used as a pesticide spray (Diervorst, Oct 2016).

In most of the cases, smart toilet hubs in government schools or rural and urban slum areas are being set up through CSR partnerships or via public–private partnerships with government bodies (Idle, Jan 2019).

Besides smart sanitation solutions, GARV Toilets offers an integrated water, sanitation, and hygiene solution in the form of GARV Smart Sanitation Centres. This integrated offering includes smart GARV Toilets, bath facilities, water ATMs, laundry setup, and a business kiosk for health and hygiene-related products and services (GARV Website, 2019). The setup for GARV Smart Sanitation Centres includes the following steps and activities. GARV Toilets enters into a long-term public–private partnership (PPP) with an urban local body (ULB). The company requests and gets a land allocation from the government in the target region or geography. The next step involves getting an asset financer on board. Further, the company collaborates with an NGO partner and on-boards a clean team for ensuring cleanliness, hygiene, and timely maintenance. The company designs and deploys the Smart Sanitation Centre along with the advertising kiosks for advertizing-based revenues (GARV Website, 2019; Gorvett, Feb 2019). Other potential revenue streams involve pay-per-use or subscription-based models (GARV Website, 2019; WNR, 2016).

The company is able to provide a high level of maintenance at minimal cost due to automation. IoT setup enables the company and its grassroots partners to track the usage patterns of all toilets in real-time. IoT dashboard offers a diverse range of data points like breakage in infrastructure, usage patterns, and hygiene behavior of people, for example, how many are washing their hands after using the toilet, etc. Hygiene-related details are shared with local government to act upon during health education campaigns. Figure 11 provides a detailed overview regarding GARV Toilet's business model.

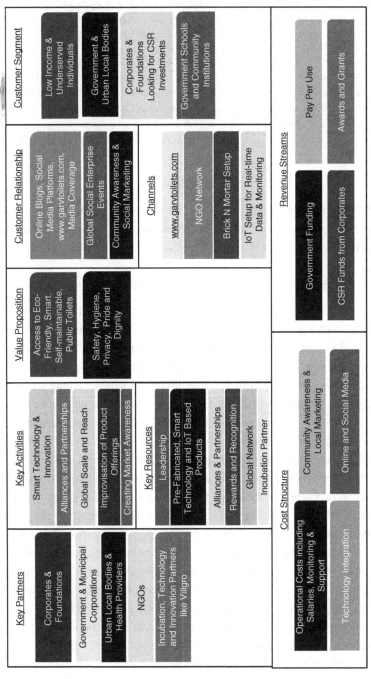

Figure 11 GARV Toilets – Business model overview

Source: Authors' creation – GARV Website (2019); Idle (Jan 2019); Gorvett (Feb, 2019); Dietvorst (Oct, 2016); Analysis done by authors in Business Model Template introduced by Osterwalder and Pigneur (2010)

4.8 BEMPU Health

I had some exposure to neonatal health while working at Embrace. I wanted to create something that would have a massive impact. If you make a difference to a baby's life, it actually affects the next 60–80 years of their life.
*– Ratul Narain, Founder, BEMPU (**BEMPU** Villgro, 2019; Sinha, Apr 2016)*

Among babies with low birth weight, infections can occur at home. Up to 15 percent of low-weight newborns discharged from government Newborn Intensive Care Unit (NICU) would die at home due to complications like infections and hypothermia ... That's what made me work on a low-cost solution.
– Ratul Narain, Founder, BEMPU (Rao, Nov 2017).

Vision and Mission

At BEMPU Health, our vision is for all children to have the chance to live full and healthy lives. To achieve this, BEMPU Health offers innovative lifesaving health products for children in low-resource areas (BEMPU Website, 2019).

What Is the Underlying Context and Background?

Globally, more than 2.5 million babies die within one month of their birth. For every three newborns having health issues like neonatal hypothermia, two babies can be saved by using simple innovations like real-time temperature monitoring and alerting applications. Many of the surviving children face long-term health issues due to lack of attention to preventable health problems during and after birth (BEMPU Website, 2019). Neonatal hypothermia affects one-third of children in India. Newly born infants weighing less than 2.5 kilograms have insufficient fat to keep their body warm. So, these infants have to spend lot of calories in maintaining their body temperature thereby not gaining weight and becoming susceptible to infection (Thomas, Jan 2019). This fat-burning process results in the by-production of acid in the baby's body, which further affects baby's breathing pattern. When baby faces difficulty in breathing, oxygen supply (hypoxia) gets cut-off and results in damage to body organs (Sinha, Apr 2016). This situation also adversely affects the IQ (intelligence quotient) level and overall development of the baby in growing years. However, due to resource challenges and as per general protocol, a newborn is considered as healthy and discharged even if it weighs 1.5 kilograms in India (Thomas, Jan 2019). This leads to health complications like hypothermia for some infants at home because generally, parents are not aware and not monitoring body temperature of infants.

Ratul Narain set up BEMPU in 2014 as a public health organization focusing on helping newborns who are underweight and at risk of getting hypothermia

(Sinha, Apr 2016). Initial funding came from the Gates Foundation. Before setting up BEMPU, Narain spent six years at Johnson & Johnson in the cardiovascular space and one year at Embrace Innovations in the neonatal health segment (**BEMPU** Villgro, 2019). In 2013, he decided to transition his career from making incremental improvements in medical devices for obese people in the USA to delivering a high-impact health product for undernourished children in developing economies like India (Dharssi, Sep 2015). Before launching BEMPU, Narain spent one year in the field looking at the major problems associated with high infant mortality rates in India as well as having interactions with more than 100 pediatricians and neonatologists across India. He observed a lack of close monitoring for infants in government hospitals, rural clinics, and homes. Some of the nurses could not read the temperature properly. Many parents could not differentiate between degrees centigrade and Fahrenheit. Kangaroo care, a procedure to keep babies warm, was not practiced properly (Dharssi, Sep 2015). He also noticed how incubators were overcrowded, with three times more high-risk babies together than the recommended numbers, and how hospitals and clinics lacked experienced staff and how overworked nurses managed high volumes of patients. Low-income parents couldn't afford to lose working days and preferred to get early release from hospital for their babies (Doshi, Nov 2016).

All these observations prompted Narain to design and launch a simple yet effective temperature-monitoring wristband, a real-time online monitoring service, a wrap for kangaroo-mother care, and other lifesaving solutions for the infants. The BEMPU wristband or bracelet monitors the infant's body temperature and raises an audio-visual alarm for the parents when body temperature falls even 0.5 degrees Celsius below the threshold level of 36.5 degree Celsius or 97.7 Fahrenheit (Rao, Nov 2017). If the baby is warm, a blue light keeps blinking every thirty seconds. If baby starts getting cold, the bracelet raises an audio-visual alarm and an orange light starts blinking. This indicates that baby is entering the state of hypothermia (Singh, Jun 2016). Timely alert results in effective monitoring and lifesaving quick action by parents or caretaker (Thomas, Jan 2019). As an initial step, caretakers are advised to hold the baby to their chest to provide kangaroo-mother care. According to World Health Organization (WHO) recommendations, if mother or father or caregiver binds the baby to their chest via a cloth, then their body heat gets transferred to the baby's body, thereby raising baby's body temperature (Thomas, Jan 2019). This technique is relatively more useful than the use of incubators. According to United Nations International Children's Emergency Fund (UNICEF) estimates, timely and effective response to hypothermia can save the lives of more than

30 percent of newborns (around one million babies) across developing countries in the first month of their lives (Dharssi, Sep 2015).

Understanding the Socioeconomic Impact

During 2014–2019, BEMPU created a global presence impacting thousands of babies across several countries. The company offers lifesaving healthcare products for infants as individual commercial offerings as well as public health deployments. BEMPU's lifesaving healthcare products for infants have helped more than 17,000 newborns in more than 241 health facilities globally. Also, BEMPU has engaged and empowered more than 1,039 health workers in creating market awareness and last-mile reach (BEMPU Website, 2019).

How Does It Operate?

Narain set up BEMPU in 2014 after spending a year in the field in India trying to understand the key reasons behind the high rate of infant mortality. During one year in the field, he spent time in various pediatric centers across government and private hospitals as well as rural clinics, interacted with different doctors and healthcare specialists, recruited a team of engineers and product designers, and finally came up with the concept of the hypothermic bracelet (Thomas, Jan 2019).

> *I hung out there to understand the life of the doctor, the life of a patient, etc. I was literally there with a notebook listing the healthcare gaps I saw – why did a baby get sick? Why did a baby arrive dead at the hospital?* – Ratul Narain, Founder, BEMPU (Sinha, Apr 2016)

The company reached thousands of babies within a year of launch and got awarded as one of the best health innovations of 2017 (Thomas, Jan 2019). The success of BEMPU in launching a novel concept is attributed to the following key success factors.

BEMPU focuses on simplicity and ease-of-usability features in innovative lifesaving product offerings for infants. BEMPU's team work closely with the target group (low-income families), doctors, hospital support staff, and caregivers and understand their problems, views, and inputs regarding the hypothermic bracelet and other offerings. At different times, the company reviewed varying inputs, feedback, and suggestions, such as Bluetooth connectivity, short messaging service (SMS) alerts, temperature display on the device, etc., and took appropriate steps to enhance the quality and usefulness of the product without making it more complicated (Sinha, Apr 2016).

We probed if we should have a temperature display on the bracelet, but it seemed to be a little more confusing to mothers. These mothers are already so worried because their babies are so sick. We decided to keep it extremely simple – blue light indicates the baby is fine, red light indicates the temperature has dropped, kicking off the beeping indicates that the baby needs assistance.

– *Ratul Narain, Founder, BEMPU (*Sinha, Apr 2016*)*

According to Narain, majority of new social enterprises face challenges in building a team, designing and marketing a novel concept, and creating last-mile connect and reach among the masses. During launch, BEMPU gained trust, support, mentoring, and funding from globally renowned agencies like United States Agency for International Development (USAID), the Bill and Melinda Gates Foundation, Siemens Foundation, Villgro, and Grand Challenges, Canada. The backing from global foundations and institutions has led to the success of BEMPU in terms of design, technology integration, launch, and marketing of the lifesaving bracelet and other high-impact product offerings (Thomas, Jan 2019).

New social enterprises face significant challenges in gaining access and acceptance among government institutions in developing economies. Lifesaving devices have significant potential to make a large-scale impact on low-income communities relying on government hospitals and primary and secondary care institutions, especially in developing economies like India. However, governments, especially in developing economies, follow a detailed due-diligence process to screen the innovations from private enterprises before giving a go-ahead for implementation in government institutions (Thomas, Jan 2019). This requires a lot of time, effort, and budget to conduct the pilots and align with the government institutions for acceptance. However, global focus and attention towards socioeconomic inequality and poverty by UN SDGs is making it relatively easier for private companies to gain acceptance for their innovations with the government institutions.

Another key challenge for a new social enterprise lies in achieving significant scale and reach. Scalability is essential for any social entrepreneurial idea to ensure financial sustainability and high social impact. BEMPU has collaborated with UNICEF to conduct pilots in different countries. The findings enable the company to fine tune their product offerings as well as achieve global scalability and reach (Thomas, Jan 2019). Figure 12 provides a detailed overview regarding BEMPU's business model.

4.9 Janitri Innovations

More than 90 percent of the maternal & newborn mortality/morbidity can be prevented by simple & innovative products in a sustainable manner.

Arun Agarwal, Founder, Janitri Innovations (Villgro Janitri, 2019*)*

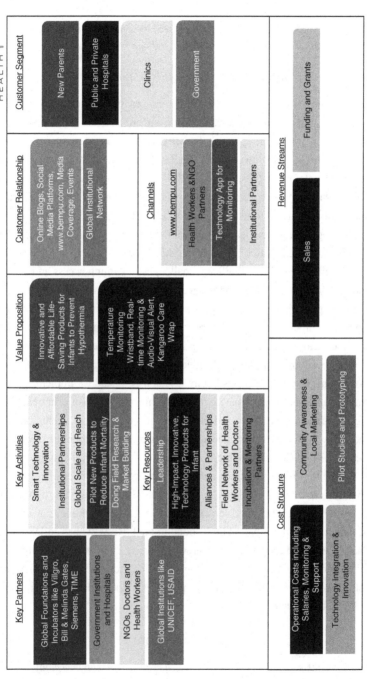

Figure 12 BEMPU Health – Business model overview

Source: Authors' creation – BEMPU Website (2019); BEMPU Thomas (Jan 2019); Villgro (2019); Rao (Nov 2017); Doshi (Nov 2016); Singh (Jun 2016); Sinha (Apr 2016); Analysis done by authors in Business Model Template introduced by Osterwalder and Pigneur (2010)

What Is the Underlying Context and Background?

Every year, more than 250,000 women die globally during the intrapartum period. Also, there are more than 1 million intrapartum stillbirths and 0.9 million intrapartum-related neonatal deaths globally (Janitri Website, 2019). The majority of these deaths are avoidable with the engagement of highly skilled nurses as well as a process for real-time monitoring during delivery and the intrapartum period. In developing economies like India, more than 80 percent of deliveries are done by staff nurses and the majority of these deliveries are being done in low-resource settings by semi-skilled nurses without making use of proper labor, fetus, and uterine contraction monitoring setups (Janitri Website, 2019; Villgro Janitri, 2019). Cardiotocography (CTG) and WHO-recommended partograph are mainly used during pregnancy for monitoring Fetal heart rate (FHR), Uterine contractions (UC) and labor monitoring respectively. CTG requires a skilled gynecologist for analyzing the FHR and UC patterns to ensure the well-being of mother and fetus (Janitri Website, 2019). Also, CTG is costly, nonportable and is dependent upon a highly skilled nurse or gynecologist for correct interpretation. Another tool, partograph, is filled up by nurses and in majority of the cases, this labor-monitoring template has been reduced to a data-recording formality after delivery, especially in regional government and private hospitals and clinics where nurses and para-medical staff are not properly trained. Partograph is complicated and can't be used effectively as a labor-monitoring tool unless and until staff is trained properly and is made accountable for correct and accurate information. Partograph does not raise any real-time alert if any anomaly is found, thereby a call-to-action depends on the nurses (Janitri Website, 2019). Labor monitoring and uterine contraction are among the key parameters, which indicate complications during the intrapartum period. Regular monitoring of these key parameters tends to get ignored due to nurses' work overload as well as early release of mother and child. Lack of proper labor and uterine contraction monitoring results in avoidable complications and morbidity for mother and child (Janitri Website, 2019; Villgro Janitri, 2019).

There is a growing demand for technology-oriented affordable and accurate medical devices and solutions, which can enable low-skilled healthcare workers provide accurate monitoring and decision support for mother and child during the intrapartum period, especially in low-resource areas (Villgro Janitri, 2019).

Arun Agarwal, a biomedical engineer, at a young age developed a passion for resolving grassroots healthcare issues via right technological solutions. He became associated with Biotechnology Industry Research Assistance Council (BIRAC) VILLGRO Social Innovation Immersion Program (SIIP) program. As a part of this program, Arun spent a year in visiting more than 100 hospitals,

Primary Health Centers (PHCs), and Community Health Centers (CHCs) across India and observed the grassroots issues resulting in high rate of maternal and infant mortality (Ramachandran, Apr 2019; Villgro Janitri, 2019). Grassroots learning and Villgro mentoring enabled Arun to launch Janitri Innovations in 2016 with the aim of developing sustainable technology solutions for mother and child health especially during the intrapartum period (Villgro Janitri, 2019).

Understanding the Socioeconomic Impact

During 2016–2019, Janitri's labor monitoring and uterine contraction technology solutions were adopted by more than 116 hospitals across 9 states in India. These solutions have been used to monitor more than 25,370 pregnancies during 2016–2019 (Janitri Website, 2019).

How Does It Operate?

In 2015–2016, Janitri launched Janitri Innovations as a social enterprise focusing on sustainable technology solutions for health care of mothers and infants during and after pregnancy.

During launch, Arun hired interns and conducted a Proof of Concept (POC) for the FHR and UC monitoring tool (Ramachandran, Apr 2019). Successful POC led to the launch of "Keyar", a portable and noninvasive CTG device for monitoring of the baby in mother's womb and UC of the mother-to-be (Janitri Website, 2019; Ramachandran, Apr 2019). Janitri's successful launch of Keyar from POC stage to go-to-market within two to three years is considered to be much faster as than the average five to six years taken by other companies for market launch of high technology medical devices after completed POC.

This device is linked to a mobile app and can be worn around the neck, does real-time monitoring of the FHR and UC parameters via sensors, analyzes the patterns, and raises an audio-visual alert (color code/ sound) if the fetus is in distress (Janitri Website, 2019). The device displays these parameters in an easy-to-understand format for low-skilled health workers so that they can interpret and take timely action in case of anomalies. It is much cheaper than traditional CTGs made by companies like Philips and General Electric. Keyar is IOT-enabled, portable, and runs on ordinary batteries, thereby making it highly effective and useful in remote areas where mobility, availability, and affordability of traditional, bulky equipment are a challenge (Ramachandran, Apr 2019).

Preliminary results show that Keyar's performance is as good as that of the gold-standard CTG machine. The standard CTG machine is quite big and restricts the patient to the bed . . . Often, they are restless because of the labor pains, so this gives them the freedom to move around . . . It transmits the data to the mobile application for remote monitoring.
Dr Shirley George, Professor at the Department of Obstetrics and Gynecology, St John's Medical College Hospital, Bengaluru *(*Ramachandran, Apr 2019*)*

Agarwal also observed that the majority of hospitals and health centers did not comply with WHO recommendation regarding real-time monitoring and recording of vital signs during labor delivery. Nurses in the labor ward at government hospitals and health centers are overloaded with large numbers of patients and most of them are not skilled enough to do a proper recording of labor delivery data on partograph (Janitri Website, 2019; Ramachandran, Apr 2019). In many cases, partograph charts get updated after delivery leading to a risk situation for mother and child. Agarwal modified the app to help staff nurses to track and share this data in real-time with doctors. This intelligent labor monitoring tool and mobile app was named as "Daksh." (Janitri Website, 2019; Ramachandran, Apr 2019). Daksh enables nurses and other low-skilled health workers to record the vital signs of the pregnant woman, undertakes regular monitoring as per the standard intrapartum protocol, and generates auto-alerts in case of any complications using an in-built algorithm (Janitri Website, 2019). This tool allows the doctor at a remote location to do a live review of labor progress and guide the nurses for an appropriate action.

Daksh helps us keep a check on all the patients simultaneously . . . While recording the parameters manually in the partograph, errors occur sometimes, but this software has zero errors.
*Dr. Kumar Yadappanavar, from a PHC in Karnataka's Tumkur district (**Patil, Jul 2017)**

Janitri's core strength lies in focus on continuous innovation and hiring the right resources who are aligned with the company's passion to innovate and make a difference in the lives of the common people (IS, 2019). Janitri believes in a process of *"do early, fail early"* and maintains consistent focus on experimentation, conducting field-pilots, and product and process innovations (IS, 2019). During the field-pilot, Janitri's team does a real-time testing of the product or feature in rural, semi-urban, and urban hospitals and health centers, takes on-field feedback from doctors, patients, and nurses, and makes a final decision regarding go or no-go or modification in the pilot product or feature (IS, 2019). Regarding people, Janitri has hired people with diverse qualifications and expertise in areas like electronics, mechanical, design, public health, computers, and biomedical (IS, 2019).

For any organization, team matters. We are a social healthcare startup and we look for a candidate who is passionate for his/her expert area and social sector.

Arun Agarwal, Founder, Janitri Innovations *(*IS, 2019*)*

Janitri works on variable pricing models including public–private partnerships (PPP) depending upon the healthcare infrastructure and socioeconomic dynamics of the target region. It attracts grants and funding from government, corporations, and foundations as well for undertaking product innovations, conducting pilots, and enabling access to mothers-to-be from low-income and poor households. Looking at the high potential for scale and impact, Janitri has a generous grant and funding model from Government of India, Bill and Melinda Gates Foundation, Villgro, BIRAC, and governments from other countries like Canada (Janitri Website, 2019; Ramachandran, Apr 2019). Janitri is targeting ISO-13485 and IEC 60601 certifications to comply with prescribed international quality standards for medical devices (Ramachandran, Apr 2019). It is also aiming at CE (Conformité Européene) marking for the European market besides targeting South East Asia and Africa (Ramachandran, Apr 2019). Figure 13 provides a detailed overview regarding Janitri's business model.

5 Connecting the Dots: Smart Relationships and Economic Approaches

This section highlights key findings that have been derived from extensive analysis of nine social businesses targeting differentiated needs at the BoP. What kind of smart social infrastructures have been designed and implemented by the selected social businesses in BoP emerging markets? Table 4 maps the key findings to the sampled list of social businesses.

5.1 Incubation/Incubatee Relationship Matters

The review of the selected social businesses highlights the significance of early-stage funding and mentoring from experts in the success of social businesses at the BoP. There are an increasing number of social enterprises facing constraints in achieving scale, reach, and sustainability. One of the key reasons attributed to these constraints is the lack of timely funding and mentoring support to the social business start-ups during their initial years. The majority of these start-ups are driven by an idea to change the world but lack access to adequate cash flow and a professional team of experts who can design and implement a right business model to scale and sustain.

Social businesses like Villgro and Aavishkaar identified this gap as a much-needed area for action. These companies decided to develop an ecosystem that can provide end-to-end mentoring, advisory support, and early-stage

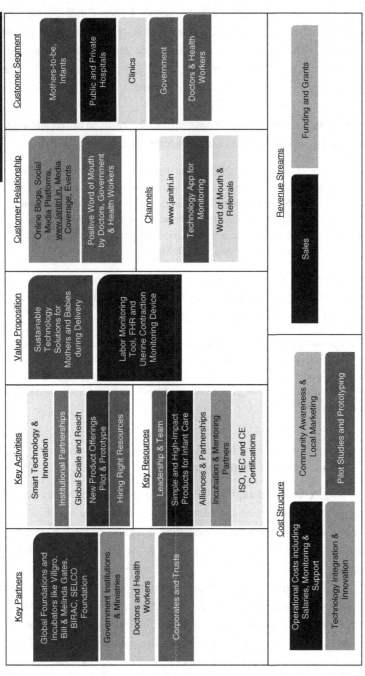

Figure 13 Janitri Innovations – Business model overview

Source: Authors' creation – Janitri Website (2019); Villgro Janitri (2019); Ramachandran (Apr 2019); IS (2019); Patil (Jul 2017); Analysis done by authors in Business Model Template introduced by Osterwalder and Pigneur (2010)

funding to social business start-ups during their initial phase of ideation, conceptualization, and market launch. Over time, many other social business incubators like Dasra, UnLtd India, Acumen Fund, Omdiyar Network, Deshpande Foundation, Rural Technology and Business Incubator (RTBI), Upaya Social Ventures, Ennovent, etc., have emerged in India. These social incubators attract, select, inspire, mentor, fund, and incubate social business start-ups to grow into self-sustainable, high-growth, and high-impact social enterprises.

An increasing number of social incubators has resulted in an increasing number of successful and self-sustainable social businesses at the BoP.

> Sandeep Patel, Cofounder & CEO, Nepra Resource Management Pvt. Ltd said, *"We have been fortunate to have an investor like Aavishkaar who empowered us with capital when other investors were unwilling given our small size and rudimentary operations. We have benefited significantly from their unflinching support, guidance and networks in transforming our vision into a scalable business."* (Empea, Oct 2018)

Similarly, a number of social businesses in diverse need segments, including sanitation, hygiene, and healthcare, like GARV Toilets, BEMPU, and Janitri Innovations have been incubated by Villgro.

> Anupam Sinhal, Founder, BookmyBai said, *"Villgro is a rare combination of capital and mentoring, both of which are extremely important for a startup. Unlike any other accelerator, it helps in grooming the company, helping it at every step of the way, through guidance and exposure to industry experts."* (Barua, Aug 2019).

5.2 Innovative Funding Models Like Crowdfunding and Impact Investing Creating a Difference

Access to long-term social capital is considered to be one of the key decisive factors in growth and sustainability of social businesses. However, there exists a wide gap in terms of expectations and beliefs of the social business entrepreneurs versus financial institutions and investors. At one end, social business entrepreneurs look at a self-sustainable social mission as a primary driver while targeting the BoP segment. This implies designing and offering high-quality and affordable product and service solutions to the BoP segment at low margins. In this scenario, significant time and capital go into market building, creating trust and awareness, as well as product and service prototyping. Gradually, this results in adoption by the target segment at the BoP, and generates revenue. However, financial institutions and investors are not willing to lend long-term capital for these kinds of businesses and look at social business as they look at any other investment opportunity, namely that it should yield economic gains as soon as possible.

This conflict in priorities leads to either dilution of the social mission or failure of the social business enterprise. Since early 2000, there has been a gradual entry of social incubators as well as the launch of social financial engineering platforms that tackle the mission conflict with commercial investors via innovative funding streams and models. **Crowdfunding** is one of these models where social businesses themselves develop an online technology platform to reach individual investors and raise low-cost funds from micro-investors rather than banks or large investors. Here, micro-investors are a specific set of individuals who are willing to invest in a social idea or contribute to a social business with nominal returns. Crowdfunding technology platforms like Rang De, Ketto, Kickstarter, Milaap, etc., act as smart social business platforms where a direct interface exists between lenders (individual micro-investors) and BoP target segment (micro-enterprises and households). Here, the BoP target segment is looking for access to low-cost funding to address an immediate business need or family challenge. Crowdfunding platforms bridge the complexities and underlying challenges of give and take such as identifying the right causes, trust deficit, donor apathy, and timely access to low-cost funding.

> Regarding Rang De launch, N K Ramakrishna, Cofounder, Rang De said, *"Muhammed Yunus won the Nobel Peace Prize and that's when we stumbled upon the concept of microcredit. We realized that interest rates in the space were exorbitant and borrowers in Andhra Pradesh had committed suicides because of their inability to pay loans. That's when the idea of Rang De was born using microcredit to help people in need."* (Gupta, Sep 2016)

5.3 Digital Ecosystem Is Becoming a Key Enabler to Transform Lives at the BoP

The continuous advancement, adoption, and penetration of digital technologies has played a significant role in ensuring a last-mile connect and reach to the BoP segment residing in rural and semi-urban areas. As of 2018–2019, there are more than 5.11 billion unique mobile users and 4.39 billion Internet users in the world.[9] With every passing year, ICT is becoming more integrated, speed and quality of communication is getting better, and cost of ownership and usage charges are decreasing due to hyper-competition and mass usage (Smith et al., 2011).

The increasing advancement, accessibility, and affordability of ICT have resulted in socioeconomic transformation at the BoP. **Financial inclusion is one of the areas** where ICT penetration has played a significant role in enabling

---

[9] https://datareportal.com/reports/digital-2019-global-digital-overview (last accessed 11 Nov 2019).

last-mile access to financial services for the BoP segment like m-banking, remittances, microfinance, crowdfunding, and crop insurance. A few related examples at the BoP include Safaricom in Kenya, Airtel Pay in Africa, Rang De in India, and Grameen Telecom in Bangladesh. **Another key impact** area relates to last-mile reach/connect and sales and distribution where digital platforms (mobile and internet) have enabled the direct interface between suppliers and buyers without the need for intermediaries. Related examples include redBus providing online inter-state travel booking services in India, Skymet delivering weather forecasts to farmers, and ekGaon Technologies offering technology-enabled services like direct cash or benefit transfer, etc., through mobile phones to rural and semi-urban communities. Another benefit of ICT adoption involves enabling online access to public services like online education, sanitation, telemedicines and other e-governance services. This saves significant time and efforts for BoP individuals. E-governance projects by state governments in India, like Andhra Pradesh's e-governance initiative, have yielded significant socioeconomic gains for the BoP segment.

Another key benefit of ICT adoption is seen in enabling access to critical healthcare for infants and mothers living in semi-urban and rural areas. For example, BEMPU offers an integrated technology-based temperature monitoring solution for infants comprising a real-time monitoring wristband and audio-visual alerts facility.

> **Ratul Narain, Founder, BEMPU** said, *"In the US, a hospital would keep an underweight baby in an incubator until the baby is at a healthy weight and only then discharge the baby. While in India, low birthweight babies are discharged even at 1.2 kg. These babies are at high risk for many issues, two of which are hypothermia and infections. We're not a replacement for an incubator, but we offer thermal protection via thermal monitoring of these babies . . . [via a simple real-time monitoring bracelet]."* (Sinha, April 2016)

Similarly, **Janitri** offers cost-effective technology solutions for real-time monitoring of vital parameters in infants and mothers during delivery.

> **Arun Agarwal, Founder, Janitri Innovations** said, *"More than 90 percent of the maternal and newborn mortality/morbidity can be prevented by simple and innovative products in a sustainable manner."* (Villgro Janitri, 2019)

Environmental sustainability is another impact area where the increasing role of ICT has contributed in minimizing the harmful effects of environmental pollution. Digital technologies are increasingly being used for creating innovative solutions to address the challenges of carbon emissions and global warming. Companies like Chakr Innovation and Phool are leveraging technology-based innovations to control pollution at source and recycle flower waste respectively.

5.4 Go Circular Is Emerging as a Differentiator between Success and Failure at the BoP

During data collection and analysis as a part of this study, it is observed that circular, sharing, and service-oriented business models are gaining attention and transforming the traditional ownership-driven buyer–seller ecosystem. A similar trend is observed during the BoP 3.0 literature review. Globally, enterprises are looking at environmental impact as one of the key decisive factors during the design and implementation of their business models. Circular economy demands deep-dive and higher order engagement of the customers in diverse roles and responsibilities – consumers, value cocreators, campaigners, micro-entrepreneurs, employees, and investors (crowdfunding).

Phool, a social business, collects the flower waste from religious places followed by processing and recycles it into organic incense, vermicompost, and biodegradable packaging. At one end, this has created a socioeconomic opportunity for low-income women. At another end, this has led to a significant reduction in pesticide contamination of the river Ganges.

Ankit Agarwal, Cofounder, Phool said, *"When we started three years ago, it was a simple exercise to make use of the enormous temple waste generated in our region. But today it has become a movement of sorts: we have many people experimenting in their own cities and working on replicating our model. It's a time-consuming process but we are glad it has started a dialogue on the issue . . . Our priority is not just cleaning the Ganges, but also empowering local women."* (Adlakha, Sep 2018)

Similarly, **NEPRA,** another social business, facilitates corporations and industries in go-green and recycling efforts by undertaking the systemic collection, segregation, and recycling of solid waste including paper, plastic, glass, etc. This has resulted in a significant positive impact ecologically and environmently by reducing CO_2 emissions, consumption of trees, water, energy and oil, etc.

Sandeep Patel, founder, NEPRA said, *"Waste management in India needs radical changes in attitude of the generators and I think this technology enabled initiatives will help . . . The idea was to create a business model around the rag-pickers, making them an indispensable part of the business."* (Dutta, Oct 2013)

5.5 Together We Can – Win-Win Collaboration, Partnerships and Networking

During the course of literature review and data analysis in this research, it is observed that partnerships, collaborations, and networking with multiple stakeholders play a significant role in the success or failure of any enterprise at the BoP. BoP 2.0 has identified collaboration and networking as a key success factor while operating at the BoP. When targeting the BoP segment, the majority of the social enterprises have highlighted the following key challenges. How will the enterprise create awareness, trust, and acceptance among BoP individuals who have been relying on an informal market setup with scarce resources as a way of life? How will the enterprise manage to sustain with access to limited cash flow, as funding options having a social orientation are limited? How will the enterprise manage last-mile communication, delivery, distribution, and support, especially in semi-urban and rural areas? All these challenges require collaboration, partnerships, and networking with nontraditional partners including local individuals, local market competitors, CBOs, NGOs, foundations, funding and mentoring institutions like Villgro, etc. The need for collaborations, partnerships, and networking is increasing further with the growing penetration of digital technologies like internet and mobile. If we look at the sampled list of social businesses, all these enterprises have focused on collaborations and partnerships to sustain and scale their socioeconomic impact and outreach at the BoP. For different social businesses, key partners involve government and development institutions, NGOs, CBOs, social investors, CSR foundations, R&D and incubation centers, low-income individuals and communities, and self-help groups (SHGs).

Aavishkaar has developed long-term strategic partnerships with global venture capitalists and impact investors to create a pool of capital. This pool of funds is then offered to social start-ups as early-stage risk capital in the form of equity, debt, and micro-financing options. At one end, this facilitates the expansion of the social business landscape with new social start-ups tackling BoP needs. At another end, Aavishkaar acts a funnel to channel investor funds into socioeconomic ideas and generate social goodwill and economic returns for the investors.

Peter van Mierlo, CEO, FMO, the Dutch Entrepreneurial Development Bank said, *"With this investment, we hope to help the Aavishkaar Group reduce the vulnerability of India's, South East Asia's and Africa's low-income population. We have seen their enterprise-based development approach work as Limited Partners in the Aavishkaar capital side and now along with Triodos, Shell Foundation and TIAA/Nuveen we will be part of the entire group's journey . . . Vineet Rai and his team have a terrific record of finding innovative solutions to help solve many of the key social and environmental issues of our day. We look forward to growing our relationship with these world-class social entrepreneurs." (Bhalla, Sep 2019)*

Similarly, BEMPU has formed collaborations and partnerships at different levels ranging from creating market awareness, trust, and acceptance as well as scaling the impact and outreach of their infant healthcare offerings. One of the critical steps in healthcare offerings involves experimentation, prototyping, and generation of publishable clinical evidence before going ahead with mass production. Last-mile partnerships with NGOs and local individuals play an important role in data collection, field-pilots, and awareness building.

Annika Gage, International Key Account Manager, BEMPU said, *"We are now partnering with clinical institutions and NGOs that are highly experienced."* (Rao, May 2019)

GARV Toilets has developed a partnership ecosystem with diverse stakeholders including corporates, CSR foundations, government and municipal corporations, urban local bodies, NGOs, incubation, and technology and innovation partners. This collaborative network of strategic partners has enabled GARV Toilets to transform the public sanitation landscape in India, especially for low-income, underserved communities.

> **Mayank Midha, Managing Partner, GARV Toilets** said, *"Through awareness campaigns that we coordinate with our NGO partners we are also able to change the hygiene behavior of the communities we work with."* (GARV Website, 2019)

6 Limitations and Future Directions

Elements research has been limited to in-depth evaluation of social businesses in India on the basis of published information available online in the public domain. The findings from this Elements study can be enhanced further by extending the scope with primary field studies of social businesses. Also, it is recommended to extend Elements research to social businesses in other countries, especially developing and underdeveloped nations in Africa, Asia, Eastern Europe, and South America. Differentiated sociocultural, demographic, and economic setup play an important role in setting up smart social infrastructure and growth of social businesses in different countries.

An attempt has been made to include the majority of the social businesses making use of smart social infrastructures in addressing primary underserved needs like access to mentoring, healthcare, recycling, banking, funding, sanitation, and clean drinking water at the BoP. However, there are other sets of underserved needs like access to affordable housing, clean transportation, education, and clean energy where smart social infrastructures play an important role. It is recommended to extend the scope of Elements research to these remaining underserved needs in India and other countries.

Table 4 Smart Social Infrastructure – Key Findings

Enterprise	Incubatee/incubator	Social financial engineering – impact/crowfunding	Leverage technology	Collaboration and networking	Circular economy – reduce, recycle, reuse
Villgro (2001)	1. Providing end-to-end mentoring, funding, and support ecosystem for early-stage social entrepreneurs from ideation into sustainable social enterprises	1. Pooling funds from global impact investors and investing into for-profit social business ideas		1. Network of government institutions, industry experts, venture capitalists for mentoring 2. Investment partners 3. CSR foundations and corporates for seed funding	
Aavishkaar	1. Offering end-to-end advisory support and early-stage funding to social business ideas	1. Investing funds from global impact investors into social business opportunities and generating socioeconomic returns		1. Government and development institutions 2. Investment partners 3. Social businesses alumni network for mentoring the new start-ups	

Rang De (2006)	1. Providing social peer-to-peer crowdfunding platform linking individual social investors and low-income individuals seeking micro-credit at BoP	1. Integrated online technology platform for peer-to-peer crowdfunding	1. CBOs as field impact partners 2. Network of individual investors	
Phool (2015)		1. Focus on R&D and technology innovation 2. R&D setup at IIT Kanpur incubation center 3. Flowercycling and Florafoam technologies	1. R&D, innovation and incubation partners 2. Investment partners 3. Government 4. Engaging low-income women as employees – social and economic empowerment 5. Collaboration with religious institutions	1. Recycling flower waste from religious places into organic incense, vermicompost, and biodegradable packaging
Let's Recycle (Nepra) (2012)	1. Mentoring and funding support from Aavishkaar	1. Integration fleet management systems for real-time fleet	1. Network of waste pickers – social and economic empowerment	1. Connecting dry-waste generators and collectors to waste-recyclers

Table 4 (cont.)

Enterprise	Incubatee/incubator	Social financial engineering – impact/crowdfunding	Leverage technology	Collaboration and networking	Circular economy – reduce, recycle, reuse
			monitoring and optimization	2. Municipal corporations 3. Network of industries and CSR foundations	2. Technology-enabled fleet scheduling and monitoring to reduce CO_2 emissions 3. Zero waste to landfill by converting mixed waste as refuse-derived fuel to be used by cement companies
Piramal Sarvajal (2008)			1. Clean water technology IoT and cloud-based technology setup 2. Integrated technology setup for real-time usage and adoption patterns, solar-	1. Government and municipal corporations CSR foundations and corporates 2. Local governing bodies and health providers 3. Network of localized micro-entrepreneurs	

		powered water ATMs, monitoring and support setup		
GARV Toilets (2015)	1. Mentoring and funding support from Villgro	1. Pre-fabricated public toilets making use of smart technologies like IoT, RFID, LEDs, solar energy, and biodigester tanks. 2. Integrated technology setup for real-time usage and adoption patterns, monitoring and support	1. Government and municipal corporations CSR foundations and corporates 2. Urban local bodies and health providers 3. NGOs 4. Incubation, innovation and technology partners	1. Access to eco-friendly, smart, self-maintainable public toilets thereby preventing open defecation, health and environment issues 2. Wastewater recycling and solar energy setup
BEMPU (2014)	1. Mentoring and funding support from Villgro	1. Integrated technology-based offering for infants	1. Government institutions and hospitals	

Table 4 (cont.)

Enterprise	Incubatee/ incubator	Social financial engineering – impact/crowfunding	Leverage technology	Collaboration and networking	Circular economy – reduce, recycle, reuse
			comprising real-time temperature monitoring wristband and audio-visual alerting to parents.	2. Global foundations and development institutions like UNICEF, USAID 3. NGOs 4. Incubation, innovation and technology partners	
Janitri (2017)	1. Mentoring and funding support from Villgro		1. Cost-effective and real-time technology solutions for mothers and babies during delivery including labor monitoring tool, fetal heart rate, and uterine contraction monitoring devices.	1. Government institutions and hospitals 2. Global foundations, trusts, corporates, and development institutions like UNICEF, USAID 3. NGOs, doctors and health workers 4. Incubation, innovation, and technology partners	

7 Conclusion

We can confidently say that the twenty-first century has been a game-changer for the people, planet, and profits globally. During 2001–2019, the global population increased from 6.1 billion to 7.7 billion.[10] According to United Nations statistics, the world population is expected to reach 8.6 billion in 2030, 9.8 billion in 2050, and 11.2 billion in 2100 (UNDESA, June 2017). The growing number of people on this earth, primarily in developing nation implies increasing consumption of resources. Moreover, the increasing pace of industrialization and mobility patterns has led to a use-and-throw culture thereby increasing ecological and environmental stress. Despite all the technology advancements, increasing CSR spending by corporates, growing number of NGOs, deepening focus of the governments and global development institutions on pro-poor and pro-development initiatives, the socioeconomic imbalance is getting wider between developed and developing economies.

This is one side of the coin. On the flip side, during twenty-first century, there has been a positive shift, acknowledgment, and orientation among global development institutions and nations towards restoring the socioeconomic and environmental balance by coming together and framing common goals and objectives. A significant number of pro-social individuals across for-profit businesses, government entities, NGOs, and development institutions are taking the initiative either individually or together to design and develop sustainable and cleaner solutions for the people, society, and environment.

New focus areas and frontiers of the global economy have taken shape where social and environmental outcomes, along with economic performance, are considered to be collective parameters for success or failure of the businesses. This has led to the emergence of new models of entrepreneurship namely for-profit social businesses. These new models are driven by problem-solving social innovators who are in turn driven by social and environmental missions beyond economic gains. Sustainability and overall success of social businesses is driven by smart social infrastructure comprising availability of incubation ecosystems for social start-ups, access to long-term capital, availability of digital ecosystems, adoption of circular business models, and focus on collaborations, partnerships, and networking with diverse stakeholders (Figure 14).

Access to long-term capital (impact investing) as well as mentoring from industry, policy, and investment experts is one of the key enablers for the overall success of social businesses. The majority of start-up social businesses fail due to scarcity of cash flow as well as lack of expert advice, right direction, and mentoring during the initial phase of launch. Social business start-ups need

---

[10] www.worldometers.info/world-population/world-population-by-year/ (last accessed 17 Nov 2019).

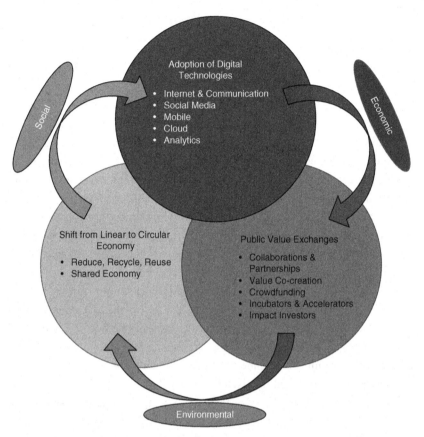

Figure 14 Smart social ecosystem at BoP

to commit significant resources (time, manpower, and capital) to creating market awareness, trust, and acceptance at the BoP. During early-stage, social business start-ups do not have sustainable revenue streams. Moreover, these start-ups have a high risk of failure due to lack of awareness regarding the appropriate go-to-market strategy. What business model to follow? How to arrange funding? Who will be the key resources? What will be the key activities? How to set up channels for last-mile connect and reach? How to build customer awareness and relationships? How to hire the right resources for operating in rural and semi-urban areas? When and how to train and engage local individuals? Companies like Villgro, Aavishkaar, and others have made a significant contribution in creating a mentoring ecosystem for social business start-ups. At one end, this has reduced the risk of failure for the social business start-ups. At other end, this has motivated the launch of more and more social businesses targeting underserved societal and environmental needs.

Increasing launch of public-value exchanges or crowdfunding platforms is another key feature towards setting up a smart social infrastructure at the BoP. Rise of public-value exchanges or crowdfunding platforms like Rang De, Milaap, MicroGraam, and others have enabled socially conscious citizens to invest in social entrepreneurs as well as micro-entrepreneurs. Access to low-cost funds without collateral has made a significant impact in the lives of BoP micro-entrepreneurs and individuals looking for immediate cash flow to resolve their urgent business or personal needs. Also, crowdfunding platforms are acting as an attractive source of low-cost capital for the social start-ups looking at early-stage seed funding.

Increasing adoption of Internet and communication technologies is identified as another key focus area that has enhanced the collaboration, agreement, and action orientation towards elimination of poverty and environmental disorders. In fact, digital technologies are reshaping social business models aimed at the environmental challenges and underserved social needs of the BoP segment. In 2019, more than 67 percent of the global population is online with access to the Internet and around 67 percent of the global population has access to mobile communication.[11] As more and more people are coming online irrespective of their socioeconomic status, last-mile reach and connectivity with the BoP segment is becoming easier than before for social enterprises. Social businesses like Phool, Nepra, BEMPU, Janitri, Rang De, GARV Toilets, and Sarvajal have leveraged digital technologies and innovations to design and implement scalable business models at the BoP.

Smart recycling, reuse, and shared economy models are identified as the next key element in smart social infrastructure setup at the BoP. Increasing numbers of enterprises, governments, development institutions, and individuals are making a conscious attempt to make a shift from linear economy (use-and-throw) to circular economy (reduce-reuse-recycle) models. Global dynamics like rapidly growing population, increasing rate of depletion of resources, and growing environmental pollution have created a sense of urgency and concern among governments, enterprises, development institutions, and individuals. Increasing numbers of social businesses like Phool, Nepra, GARV Toilets, and others have designed their business models around recycling and reuse principles, thereby making a significant positive impact on the society, ecology, and environment.

A final element of smart social infrastructure at the BoP involves **focusing on collaborations, partnerships, and networking**. Social businesses,

---

[11] wearesocial.com/blog/2019/01/digital-2019-global-internet-use-accelerates (last accessed 17 Nov 2019).

government, development institutions, technology and R&D setups, incubators, CSR foundations, NGOs, micro-entrepreneurs, and BoP individuals are coming together to cocreate, design, and deliver innovative value offerings for the underserved needs of the BoP segment. Social businesses like Phool, Nepra, Sarvajal, Janitri, BEMPU, and others have collaborated with diverse stakeholders to create high-performance, low-cost solutions for the BoP segment; build market awareness, trust, and acceptance at the BoP; as well as for scaling the impact and reach.

To **summarize**, social impact and environmental outcomes have become the new form of currency and source of competitive differentiation for enterprises today. Social enterprises are gaining recognition and acceptance as game-changers with a potential to bring a positive impact in the lives of the millions at the BoP. Today's generation especially the youth values and gets attracted to these mission-focused enterprises. Smart social infrastructure coupled with a digital ecosystem is acting as a catalyst for the entry of new social start-ups, as well as scalability and sustainability of existing social enterprises.

Abbreviations

5A's	Affordable, Accessible, Available, Acceptable, Awareness
APR	Annual Percentage Rate
ATM	Automated Teller Machine
ATP	Ability to Pay
AUM	Asset under Management
BIRAC	Biotechnology Industry Research Assistance Council
BM	Business Models
BoP	Base of the Pyramid
BRICS	Brazil, Russia, India, China, and South Africa
CALM	Community Awareness and Local Marketing
CBOs	Community-Based Organizations
CEC	Circular Economy
CO_2	Carbon Dioxide
CE	Conformité Européene
CHCs	Community Health Centers
CSR	Corporate Social Responsibility
CTG	Cardiotocography
EMF	Ellen MacArthur Foundation
ERP	Enterprise Resource Planning
FHR	Fetal Heart Rate
GIAN	Grassroots Innovation Augmentation Network
GPRS	General Packet Radio Service
ICTs	Information & Communication Technologies
IIT	Indian Institute of Technology
IoT	Internet of Things
IQ	Intelligence Quotient
KFAs	Key Focus Areas
kWh	Kilowatt-hour
LCB	Local Capacity Building
LED	Light Emitting Diode
LIS	Low-Income States
MDG	Millennium Development Goals
MFIs	Micro Financing Institutions
MIS	Management Information System
MRF	Material Recovery Facility
MSMEs	Medium, Small and Micro Enterprises

MSW	Municipal Solid Waste
MT	Metric Tonnes
NBFCs	Nonbanking Financial Companies
NGOs	Nongovernment Organization(s)
NPK	Nitrogen-Phosphorus-Potassium
NPOs	Nonprofit Organizations
P2P	Peer-to-Peer
PH	Potential of Hydrogen
PHCs	Primary Health Centers
POC	Proof of Concept
PPM	Parts Per Million
PPP	Purchasing Power Parity
R&D	Research & Development
RBI	Reserve Bank of India
RFD	Refuse-Derived Fuel
RFID	Radio Frequency Identification
SEs	Social Enterprise(s)
SEMS	Sarvajal Enterprise Management System
SHGs	Self-Help Groups
SIIP	Social Innovation Immersion Program
SMS	Short Messaging Service
UC	Uterine Contractions
UNICEF	United Nations International Children's Emergency Fund
UN SDGs	United Nations Sustainable Development Goals
USAID	United States Agency for International Development
USD	US Dollars
WHO	World Health Organization
WTP	Willingness to Pay

References

Aavishkaar Website. (2019). www.aavishkaar.in (last accessed 8 Sep 2019).

Adlakha, N. (22 Sep 2018). Recycling temple waste along the Ganges with Help Us Green. *The Hindu.* www.thehindu.com/life-and-style/the-worlds-first-biodegradable-thermocol-and-flower-leather-by-ankit-agarwals-kanpur-based-organisation-help-us-green/article25013953.ece (last accessed 16 February 2020).

AIR. (2018). Aavishkaar Impact Report 2018. www.aavishkaar.in/images/download/publications/Aavishkaar_Impact_Report_2018.pdf (last accessed 8 Sep 2019).

Alexander, S., & Padmanabhan, V. (18 Mar 2019). *Under NDA, More Toilets, Less Open Defecation.* www.livemint.com/news/india/under-nda-more-toilets-less-open-defecation-1552842931107.html (last accessed 19 Oct 2019).

Anderson, J. (2006). A structured approach for bringing mobile telecommunications to the world's poor. *The Electronic Journal of Information Systems in Developing Countries*, 27(1), 1–9.

Anderson, J., & Markides, C. (2007). Strategic Innovation at the Base of the Economic Pyramid. *MIT Sloan Management Review*, 49(1), 83–88.

Arbnor, I., & Bjerke, B. (2008). *Methodology for Creating Business Knowledge* (3rd ed.). London: Sage Publications Ltd.

Austin, J. E., Stevenson, H., & Wei-Skillern, J. (2006). Social and Commercial Entrepreneurship: Same, Different, or Both? *Entrepreneurship Theory & Practice*, 30(1), 1–22.

Banerjee, A. V., & Duflo, E. (2007). The Economic Lives of the Poor. *Journal of Economic Perspectives*, 21(1), 141–167.

Barua, A. (14 August 2019). *Rapid Infection Detection to Unbreakable Toilets: 5 Startups That are Building a Better India.* www.thebetterindia.com/191614/villgro-ipitch-startups-social-entrepreneurship-india/ (last accessed 10 Nov 2019).

BEMPU Villgro. (2019). www.villgro.org/port-bempu/ (last accessed 25 Oct 2019).

BEMPU Website. (2019). www.bempu.com (last accessed 25 Oct 2019).

Bhalla, S. S. (30 June 2018). India is Middle Income Now: Raise the Poverty Line. *The Indian Express.* https://indianexpress.com/article/opinion/columns/india-is-middle-income-now-raise-the-poverty-line-5239269/ (last accessed 1 Dec 2019).

Bhalla, T. (25 Sep 2019). *Aavishkaar Group Raises $37M from Dutch Entrepreneurial Development Bank FMO.* https://yourstory.com/2019/09/

aavishkaar-group-dutch-entrepreneur-development-bank-fmo (last accessed 17 Nov 2019).

Bhalla, T. (26 Aug 2019). [Funding alert] AI-Powered Edtech Startup Blackboard Radio Raises Seed Round from Villgro, Others. https://yours tory.com/2019/08/funding-ai-edtech-startup-blackboard-radio-villgro-learn ing (last accessed 1 Sep 2019).

Britz, J. (2004). To Know or Not to Know? A Moral Reflection on Information Poverty. *Journal of Information Science*, 30(3), 192–204.

Bugg-Levine, A., Kogut, B., & Kulatilaka, N. (2012). A New Approach to Funding Social Enterprises. *Harvard Business Review*, 90(1/2), 118–123.

CDCP. (April 2016). Global WASH Fast Facts. *Centers for Disease Control and Prevention*. www.cdc.gov/healthywater/global/wash_statistics.html (last accessed 26 Nov 2019).

Chakraborty, S. (8 Feb 2018). *Ankit Agarwal & Karan Rastogi: Saving the Ganga by Recycling Floral Waste*. www.forbesindia.com/article/30-under-30–2018/ankit-agarwal-karan-rastogi-saving-the-ganga-by-recycling-floral-waste/49369/1 (last accessed 22 Sep 2019).

Chambers, R. (1997). *Whose Reality Counts? Putting the First Last*. London: ITDG Publishing.

Chaskin, R. J., Brown, P., Venkatesh, S., & Vidal, A. (2001). *Building Community Capacity*. New Brunswick, NJ: Aldine Transaction.

Chell, E. (2007). Social Enterprise and Entrepreneurship towards a Convergent Theory of the Entrepreneurial Process. *International Small Business Journal*, 25(1), 5–26.

Chesbrough, H. (2010). Business Model Innovation: Opportunities and Barriers. *Long Range Planning*, 43(2–3), 354–363.

Chmielewski, D. A., Dembek, K., & Beckett, J. R. (2020). 'Business Unusual': Building BoP 3.0. *Journal of Business Ethics*, 161(1), 211–229.

Cosic, M. (29 March 2017). *'We Are All Entrepreneurs': Muhammad Yunus on Changing the World, One Microloan at a Time*. www.theguardian.com/sustain able-business/2017/mar/29/we-are-all-entrepreneurs-muhammad-yunus-on-changing-the-world-one-microloan-at-a-time (last accessed 2 Dec 2019).

CS Global Wealth Databook. (2018). Global Wealth Databook 2018. *Credit Suisse Research Institute*. www.credit-suisse.com/media/assets/corporate/docs/about-us/research/publications/global-wealth-databook-2018.pdf (last accessed 26 Nov 2019).

CS Global Wealth Report. (2010). Global Wealth Report 2010. *Credit Suisse Research Institute*. www.credit-suisse.com/media/assets/corporate/docs/about-us/research/publications/credit-suisse-global-wealth-report.pdf (last accessed 26 Nov 2019)

CS Global Wealth Report. (2017). Global Wealth Report 2017. *Credit Suisse Research Institute.* www.credit-suisse.com/media/assets/corporate/docs/about-us/research/publications/global-wealth-report-2017-en.pdf (last accessed 26 Nov 2019).

CS Global Wealth Report. (2018). Global Wealth Report 2018. *Credit Suisse Research Institute.* www.credit-suisse.com/media/assets/corporate/docs/about-us/research/publications/global-wealth-report-2018-en.pdf (last accessed 26 Nov 2019).

CS Global Wealth Report. (2019). Global Wealth Report 2019. *Credit Suisse Research Institute.* www.credit-suisse.com/media/assets/corporate/docs/about-us/research/publications/global-wealth-report-2019-en.pdf (last accessed 26 Nov 2019).

Dahan, N. M., Doh, J. P., Oetzel, J., & Yaziji, M. (2010). Corporate–NGO Collaboration: Co-creating New Business Models for Developing Markets. *Long Range Planning, 43*(2–3),326–342.

Dandapani, S. (30 Nov 2017). *Unpaid and Undervalued: How India's Waste Pickers Fight Apathy to Keep Our Cities Clean.* www.thenewsminute.com/article/oppressed-and-unrecognised-life-waste-pickers-crucial-india-s-sanitation-72426 (last accessed 29 Sep 2019).

Dees, J. G. (2017). The Meaning of Social Entrepreneurship. In *Case Studies in Social Entrepreneurship and Sustainability* (pp. 34–42). Routledge.

Dees, J. G., & Anderson, B. B. (2003). For-Profit Social Ventures. *International Journal of Entrepreneurship Education, 2*(1), 1–26.

DG. (22 March 2019). *An Infographic on the Drinking Water Challenge in India.* http://delhigreens.com/2019/03/22/an-infographic-on-the-drinking-water-challenge-in-india/ (last accessed 6 Oct 2019).

Dharssi, A. (23 Sep 2015). *Ratul Anand and His Baby-Saving Thermometer.* www.ozy.com/rising-stars/ratul-narain-and-his-baby-saving-thermometer/62945/#m10g01t20w15 (last accessed 25 Oct 2019).

Diervorst, C. (6 Oct 2016). *Indestructible and Smart: Public Toilet Innovation in India.* www.ircwash.org/blog/indestructible-and-smart-public-toilet-innovation-india (last accessed 19 Oct 2019).

Doshi, V. (20 Nov 2016). *Baby Bracelet Aims to Save Newborns in India from Hypothermia.* www.theguardian.com/sustainable-business/2016/nov/20/baby-bracelet-save-newborns-india-hypothermia (last accessed 25 Oct 2019).

Dutta, V. (11 Oct 2013). *NEPRA Resource Management: How Technology is Helping Waste Recycling Startup to Increase Revenues.* https://economictimes.indiatimes.com/small-biz/startups/nepra-resource-management-how-technology-is-helping-waste-recycling-startup-to-increase-revenues/articleshow/23929055.cms (last accessed 12 Nov 2019).

Eisenhardt, K. (1989). Building Theories from Case Study Research. *The Academy of Management Review*, 14(4), 532–550

Eisenhardt, K. M., & Melissa, E. G. (2007). Theory Building from Cases: Opportunities and Challenges. *Academy of Management Journal*, 50(1), 25–32.

EIU. (December 2007). *Path to Growth: The Power of Technology in Emerging Markets*, http://graphics.eiu.com/upload/Cisco_Path_to_Growth.pdf (last accessed 2 June 2019).

Empea. (Oct 2018). *Case Study: Nepra Resource Management Pvt. Ltd.* www.empea.org/app/uploads/2018/10/CaseStudy_Nepra_WEB.pdf (last accessed 29 Sep 2019).

Esposito, M., Kapoor, A., & Goyal, S. (2012). Enabling Healthcare Services for the Rural and Semi-urban Segments in India: When Shared Value Meets the Bottom of the Pyramid. *Corporate Governance*, 12(4), 514–533.

ET. (8 Jan 2014). *Online Microfinance Platform Rang De Invites Equity Investments for Social Benefit.* https://economictimes.indiatimes.com/small-biz/entrepreneurship/online-microfinance-platform-rangde-invites-equity-investments-for-social-benefit/articleshow/29459751.cms (last accessed 14 Sep 2019).

Eyring, M. J., Johnson, M. W., & Nair, H. (2011). New Business Models in Emerging Markets. *Harvard Business Review*, 89(1/2), 88–95.

GARV Website. (2019). www.garvtoilets.com (last accessed 19 Oct 2019).

Geisendorf, S., & Pietrulla, F. (2018). The Circular Economy and Circular Economic Concepts: A Literature Analysis and Redefinition. *Thunderbird International Business Review*, 60(5), 771–782.

Gibb, A., & Adhikary, D. (2000). Strategies for Local and Regional NGO Development: Combining Sustainable Outcomes with Sustainable Organizations. *Entrepreneurship and Regional Development*, 12, 137–161.

Glaser, B. G., & Strauss, A. L. (1967). The Discovery of Grounded Theory: Strategies for Qualitative Research. Chicago: Aldine.

Gorvett, Z. (8 Feb 2019). *Tackling Slums By Making Them Better Places to Live In.* www.bbc.com/future/article/20190208-tackling-slums-by-making-them-better-places-to-live-in (last accessed 19 Oct 2019).

Goyal, S. (2019). Reducing Waste in Circular Economy. In *Encyclopedia of Renewable and Sustainable Materials* (2019 ed.). UK: Elseiver. https://doi.org/10.1016/B978-0-12-803581-8.11503-6.

Goyal, S., & Sergi, B. S. (2015a). Creating a Formal Market Ecosystem for Base of the Pyramid Markets: Strategic Choices for Social Embeddedness. *International Journal of Business and Globalisation*, 15(1), 63–80.

Goyal, S., & Sergi, B. S. (2015b). Social Entrepreneurship and Sustainability: Understanding the Context and Key Characteristics. *Journal of Security & Sustainability Issues*, 4(3), 269–278.

Goyal, S., Esposito, M., & Kapoor, A. (2016). Circular Economy Business Models in Developing Economies: Lessons from India on Reduce, Recycle, and Reuse Paradigms. *Thunderbird International Business Review*, 60(5), 729–740.

Goyal, S., Esposito, M., Kapoor, A., Jaiswal, M. P., & Sergi, B. S. (2014). Linking Up: Inclusive Business Models for Access to Energy Solutions at Base of the Pyramid in India. *International Journal of Business and Globalisation*, 12(4), 413–438.

Goyal, S., Sergi, B. S., & Jaiswal, M. P. (2016). Understanding the Challenges and Strategic Actions of Social Entrepreneurship at Base of the Pyramid. *Management Decision*, 54(2), 418–440.

Goyal, S., Sergi, B. S., & Jaiswal, M. P. (2015). How to Design and Implement Social Business Models for Base-of-the-Pyramid (BoP) Markets? *The European Journal of Development Research*, 27(5), 850–867.

Goyal, S., Sergi, B. S., & Kapoor, A. (2017). Emerging Role of For-Profit Social Enterprises at the Base of the Pyramid: The Case of Selco. *Journal of Management Development*, 36(1),97–108.

Goyal, S., Sergi, B. S., & Kapoor, A. (2014). Understanding the Key Characteristics of an Embedded Business Model for the Base of the Pyramid Markets. *Economics & Sociology*, 7(4), 26–40.

Granovetter, M. S. (1985). Economic Action and Social Structure: The Problem of Embeddedness. *American Journal of Sociology*, 91(3), 481–510.

Grootaert, C., & Van Bastelaer, T. (2002). *Understanding and Measuring Social Capital: A Synthesis of Findings and Recommendations from the Social Capital Initiative*. World Bank Social Capital Initiative Working Paper No. 24. Washington, DC: World Bank.

Grootaert, C., Narayan, D., Jones, V.N., & Woolcock, M. (2004). *Measuring Social Capital: An Integrated Questionnaire*. World Bank Working Paper. No. 18, Washington, D.C.: The World Bank.

Gupta, N. (9 Sep 2016). *Add Colour to Many Lives*. Deccan Chronicle. www.deccanchronicle.com/lifestyle/viral-and-trending/090916/add-colour-to-many-lives.html (last accessed 10 Nov 2019).

Hammond, A. L., Kramer, W. J., Katz, R. S., Tran, J. T., & Walker, C. (2007). *The Next 4 Billion: Market Size and Business Strategy at the Base of the Pyramid*. Washington, DC: World Resources Institute. www.wri.org/publication/the-next-4-billion (last accessed 12 June 2019).

Hart, S. L. (2005). *Capitalism at the Crossroads: The Unlimited Business Opportunities in Solving the World's Most Difficult Problems.* Upper Saddle River, NJ: Wharton School Publishing.

Hart, S. L. & Christensen, C. M. (2002). The Great Leap: Driving Innovation from the Base of the Pyramid. *Sloan Management Review,* 44(1), 51–56.

Hart, S. L., & London, T. (2005). Developing Native Capability: What Multinational Corporations Can Learn from the Base of the Pyramid? *Stanford Social Innovation Review,* 3(2), 28–33.

Hart, S. L., & Sharma, S. (2004). Engaging Fringe Stakeholders for Competitive Imagination. *Academy of Management Executive,* 18(1), 7–18.

Idle, T. (Jan 2019). *How Smart Tech Is Bringing Toilets to the Masses Across the Developing World.* https://sustainablebrands.com/read/product-service-design-innovation/how-smart-tech-is-bringing-toilets-to-the-masses-across-the-developing-world (last accessed 19 Oct 2019).

IEA. (2017). Energy Access Outlook 2017. *International Energy Agency.* www.iea.org/access2017/ (last accessed 26 Nov 2019).

IFMR. (2011). The Base of Pyramid distribution challenge. http://ifmrlead.org/the-base-of-pyramid-distribution-challenge/ (last accessed 12 June 2019).

IS. (2019). *Janitri Innovations: Refurbishing Viable Technology to Enhance Maternal and Child Healthcare.* www.insightssuccess.in/janitri-innovations-refurbishing-viable-technology-to-enhance-maternal-and-child-healthcare/ (last accessed 26 Oct 2019).

IWP. (2019). *Solid Waste. India Water Portal.* www.indiawaterportal.org/topics/solid-waste (last accessed 29 Sep 2019).

Janitri Website. (2019). https://janitri.in/ (last accessed 26 Oct 2019).

Jose, P. D. (2008a). Rethinking the BoP: New Models for the New Millennium – Academic Perspective. *IIMB Management Review,* 20(2), 198–202.

Jose, P. D. (2008b). Rethinking the BoP: New Models for the New Millennium – Discussion. *IIMB Management Review,* 20(2), 203–214.

Kapoor, A., & Goyal, S. (2013). Inclusive Healthcare at Base of the Pyramid (BoP) in India. *International Journal of Trade and Global Markets,* 6(1), 22–39.

Karnani, A. (2007). The Mirage of Marketing to the Bottom of the Pyramid: How the Private Sector Can Help Alleviate Poverty? *California Management Review,* 49(4), 90–111.

Kepler Cheuvreux. (24 May 2013). *The Business of Social Business is Business,* www.longfinance.net/media/documents/KC_inclusivebusiness_2013.pdf (last accessed 2 June 2019).

Khan, R. (2016). How Frugal Innovation Promotes Social Sustainability. *Sustainability,* 8(10), 1034–1063.

Kondepudy, B. (5 Jul 2016). *Flower Power – Helpusgreen: Ankit Agarwal and Karan Rastogi.* www.fortuneindia.com/ideas/flower-power/100305 (last accessed 22 Sep 2019).

Kotabe, M., & Hansen, K. (2010). *Global Marketing Management* (5th ed.). USA: Wiley

Lahiry, S. (8 May 2019). *India's Challenges in Waste Management.* www .downtoearth.org.in/blog/waste/india-s-challenges-in-waste-management-56753 (last accessed 29 Sep 2019).

Letelier, M. F., Flores, F., & Spinosa, C. (2003). Developing Productive Customers in Emerging Markets. *California Management Review*, 45(4), 77–103.

London, T. (2009). Making Better Investments at the Base of the Pyramid. *Harvard Business Review*, 87(5), 106–113

London, T. (2008). The Base-of-the-Pyramid Perspective: A New Approach to Poverty Alleviation. *Academy of Management Proceedings*, 2008(1), 1–6.

London, T., & Hart, S.L. (2004). Reinventing Strategies for Emerging Markets: Beyond the Transnational Model. *Journal of International Business Studies*, 35(5), 350–370.

Luke, B., & Chu, V. (2013). Social Enterprise versus Social Entrepreneurship: An Examination of the 'Why' and 'How' in Pursuing Social Change. *International Small Business Journal, 31*(7), 764–784.

McCarthy, N. (22 June 2017). *The World's Most Populous Nations in 2050* [Infographic]. www.forbes.com/sites/niallmccarthy/2017/06/22/the-worlds-most-populous-nations-in-2050-infographic/#73deb31039f6 (last accessed 13 July 2019).

McGrath, R. G. (2010). Business Models: A Discovery Driven Approach. *Long Range Planning*, 43(2–3), 247–261.

McKinsey Global Institute. (September 2016). *Digital Finance for All: Powering Inclusive Growth in Emerging Economies*, https://mck.co/ 2MbsSSY (last accessed 2 June 2019).

MCN. (1 Jul 2018). *Aavishkaar and Asha Impact invest Rs 44 cr in Let's Recycle.* www.moneycontrol.com/news/business/startup/aavishkaar-and-asha-impact-invest-rs-44-cr-in-waste-aggregator-lets-recycle-2630651 .html. (last accessed 2 June 2019).

Meghani, V. (15 Jan 2018). *Aavishkaar-Intellecap's Vineet Rai: The forester who turned financier.* www.forbesindia.com/article/social-impact-special-2017/aavishkaarintellecaps-vineet-rai-the-forester-who-turned-financier/ 49127/1 (last accessed 8 Sep 2019).

Miles, M. B. (1979). Qualitative Data as an Attractive Nuisance: The Problem of Analysis. *Administrative Science Quarterly*, 24(4), 590–601.

Miller, D. (1996). The Embeddedness of Corporate Strategy: Isomorphism vs. Differentiation. In J. A. C. Baum & J. E. Dutton (Eds.), *Advances in Strategic Management*, 13. Greenwich, CT: JAI Press.

Nagarajan, R. (13 June 2018). *Health Spending Pushed 55 Million Indians into Poverty in a Year: Study.* https://timesofindia.indiatimes.com/india/health-spending-pushed-55-million-indians-into-poverty-in-a-year-study/article show/64564548.cms (last accessed 17 June 2019).

Nair-Ghaswalla, A. (27 May 2019). *How to Turn Waste to Wealth: Let's Recycle.* www.thehindubusinessline.com/specials/emerging-entrepreneurs/how-to-turn-waste-to-wealth-lets-recycle/article27265807.ece# (last accessed 29 Sep 2019).

Narayan, D., Chambers, R., Shah, M. K., & Petesch, P. (2000). *Crying Out for Change: Voices of the Poor.* New York: Oxford University Press

Nepra Website. (2019). www.letsrecycle.in/ (last accessed 29 Sep 2019).

Neuwirth, B. (2012). *Marketing Channel Strategies in Rural Emerging Markets.* USA: Kellogg School of Management, Northwestern University.

Osterwalder, A., & Pigneur, Y. (2010). *Business Model Generation: A Handbook for Visionaries, Game Changers, and Challengers.* USA: John Wiley & Sons.

Patil, K. (21 July 2017). *A Bengaluru Startup Aims to Take the Pain out of Pre-delivery Monitoring of Mothers-to-Be.* https://factordaily.com/janitri-pre-delivery-monitoring-partogram-daksh/ (last accessed 26 Oct 2019).

Peredo, A. M., & McLean, M. (2006). Social Entrepreneurship: A Critical Review of the Concept. *Journal of World Business*, 41(1), 56–65.

Phadke, A. (5 Dec 2018). *The Journey from Floral Waste to Fragrant Incense Sticks.* https://blog.aboutamazon.in/supporting-small-business/the-journey-from-floral-waste-to-fragrant-incense-sticks (last accessed 22 Sep 2019).

Phool Website. (2019). https://phool.co/ (last accessed 22 Sep 2019).

Pitta, D. A., Guesalaga, R., & Marshall, P. (2008). The Quest for the Fortune at the Bottom of the Pyramid: Potential and Challenges. *Journal of Consumer Marketing*, 25(7), 393–401.

Porter, M. E., & Kramer, M. R. (2011). Creating Shared Value: How to Reinvent Capitalism and Unleash a Wave of Innovation and Growth. *Harvard Business Review*, 89(1/2), 62–77.

Prahalad, C. K. (2006). The Innovation Sandbox. *Strategy+Business*, 44.

Prahalad, C. K. (2004). *The Fortune at the Bottom of the Pyramid: Eradicating Poverty through Profits.* Upper Saddle River, NJ: Wharton School Publishing.

Prahalad, C. K., & Hammond, A. (2002). Serving the World's Poor, Profitably. *Harvard Business Review*, 80(9), 48–57.

Prahalad, C. K., & Hart, S. L. (January, 2002). The Fortune at the Bottom of the Pyramid. *Strategy+Business*, 26, 54–67.

Prahalad, C .K., & Ramaswamy, V. (2006). The Co-Creation Connection. *Strategy+Business*, 27.

Prahalad, D. (Jan, 2019). The New Fortune at the Bottom of the Pyramid. *Strategy+Business*. www.strategy-business.com/article/The-New-Fortune-at-the-Bottom-of-the-Pyramid?gko=c5f11 (last accessed 16 Jun 2019).

Prahalad, D. (Spring 2019). The New Fortune at the Bottom of the Pyramid. *Strategy +Business*, (94). www.strategy-business.com/article/The-New-Fortune-at-the-Bottom-of-the-Pyramid?gko=c5f11 (last accessed 25 November 2019).

PRB. (2012). *World Population Trends 2012*. www.prb.org/world-population/ (last accessed 12 June 2019) .

PS. (22 March 2019). *Technology Helps Provide Access to Safe Drinking Water*. www.indiawaterportal.org/articles/technology-helps-provide-access-safe-drinking-water (last accessed 6 Oct 2019).

Punia, K. (4 July 2013). *Making Clean Water a Right and Reality for All – Sarvajal*. https://yourstory.com/2013/07/making-clean-water-a-right-and-reality-for-all-sarvajal (last accessed 6 Oct 2019).

PWC. (2012). *Digitization in Emerging Economies: Unleashing Opportunities at the Bottom of the Pyramid*. www.strategyand.pwc .com/media/file/Strategyand_Digitization-in-Emerging-Economies.pdf (last accessed 2 June 2019).

Rai, J. (25 Jun 2018). *Waste Management Firm Nepra Raises Series B Funding from Aavishkaar, Asha Impact*. www.vccircle.com/waste-management-firm-nepra-raises-series-b-funding-from-aavishkaar-asha-impact/ (last accessed 29 Sep 2019).

Ramachandran, S. (1 Apr 2019). *Janitri's Portable Smart Device Monitors Mother and Baby to Keep Them Safe through Childbirth*. https://yourstory.com/2019/04/janitri-babies-mothers-healthtech-device-startup (last accessed 26 Oct 2019).

Ramanujam, S. (28 May 2019). Reverse Pitch: "A Startup's Go-to-Market Strategy Needs Corporate Engagement." www.livemint.com/companies/start-ups/reverse-pitch-a-startup-s-go-to-market-strategy-needs-corporate-engagement-1559062335727.html (last accessed 1 Sep 2019).

Rang De Website. (2019). www.rangde.org/ (last accessed 15 Sep 2019).

Rangan, V. K., Chu, M., & Djorjiji P. (2011). Segmenting the Base of the Pyramid. *Harvard Business Review*, 89(6).

Rao, M. (9 May 2019). *From Stakeholder Engagement to Market Education: Success Tips for Healthtech Startups*. https://yourstory.com/2019/05/stake holder-education-healthtech-founder-investors (last accessed 17 Nov 2019).

Rao, S. (27 Nov 2017). *Bengaluru Company's Bracelet Helps Save Premature Babies.* https://timesofindia.indiatimes.com/city/bengaluru/bengaluru-companys-bracelet-helps-save-premature-babies/articleshow/61812733.cms (last accessed 25 Oct 2019).

Ridley-Duff, R. (2008). Social Enterprise as a Socially Rational Business. *International Journal of Entrepreneurial Behavior & Research, 14*(5), 291–312.

Samhita. (20XX). *Sarvajal: Water for All.* www.samhita.org/water-for-all/ (last accessed 6 Oct 2019).

Sarkar, R. (19 Apr 2018). Aavishkar-Intellecap's Vineet Rai: Diary of an Impact Investor. www.business-standard.com/article/companies/aavishkar-intellecap-s-vineet-rai-diary-of-an-impact-investor-118041900023_1.html (last accessed 8 Sep 2019).

Sarvajal Website. (2019). www.sarvajal.com/index.php (last accessed 6 Oct 2019).

Seelos, C., & Mair, J. (2005). Social Entrepreneurship: Creating New Business Models to Serve the Poor. Business Horizons, 48(3), 241–246.

Sharma, J. (19 Sep 2016). A Neoliberal Takeover of Social Entrepreneurship? Stanford Social Innovation Review. https://ssir.org/articles/entry/a_neoliberal_takeover_of_social_entrepreneurship (last accessed 23 Dec 2019).

Sharma, J. (18 Oct 2017). Avoiding the Neoliberal Trap in Social Entrepreneurship. Stanford Social Innovation Review. https://ssir.org/articles/entry/avoiding_the_neoliberal_trap_in_social_entrepreneurship# (last accessed 23 Dec 2019).

Shorrocks, A., Davies, J., & Lluberas, R. (October, 2018). *Global Wealth Report 2018.* Credit Suisse Research Institute. www.credit-suisse.com/media/assets/corporate/docs/about-us/research/publications/global-wealth-report-2018-en.pdf (last accessed 16 June 2019).

Simanis, E., & Hart, S. L. (2006). Expanding Possibilities at the Base of the Pyramid. *Innovations: Technology, Governance, Globalization, 1*(1), 43–51.

Simanis, E., & Hart, S. L. (2009). Innovation from the Inside Out. *MIT Sloan Management Review, 50*(4), 77–86.

Simanis, E., Hart, S., & Duke, D. (2008). The Base of the Pyramid Protocol: Beyond "Basic Needs" Business Strategies. *Innovations: Technology, Governance, Globalization, 3*(1), 57–84.

Singh, T. (15 June 2016). *How a Tiny Bracelet Can Save Millions of Newborn Babies Every Year in India.* www.thebetterindia.com/58347/bempu-temperature-monitoring-device-hypothermia/ (last accessed 25 Oct 2019).

Sinha, M., & Sheth, J. (2018). Growing the Pie in Emerging Markets: Marketing Strategies for Increasing the Ratio of Non-users to Users. *Journal of Business Research*, 86, 217–224.

Sinha, S. (7 April 2016). *Stanford Educated Ratul Narain Is Helping Babies Battle Hypothermia with a Simple Bracelet.* https://yourstory.com/2016/04/bempu (last accessed 25 Oct 2019).

Sinigdha, S. (15 Jan 2016). *Armed with Flowers, These Young Men from Kanpur Are on a Mission to Clean the Ganges.* https://yourstory.com/2016/01/help-us-green/ (last accessed 22 Sep 2019).

Slater, J. (11 July 2018). India Is No Longer Home to the Largest Number of Poor People in the world. Nigeria Is. *The Washington Post.* www.washingtonpost.com/news/worldviews/wp/2018/07/10/india-is-no-longer-home-to-the-largest-number-of-poor-people-in-the-world-nigeria-is/ (last accessed 1 Dec 2019).

Smith, M. L., Spence, R., & Rashid, A. T. (2011). Mobile Phones and Expanding Human Capabilities. *Information Technologies & International Development*, 7(3), 77–88.

Soto, H.D. (2000). *The Mystery of Capital: Why Capitalism Triumphs in the West and Fails Everywhere Else.* New York: Basic Books

Spence, R., & Smith, M. L. (2010). ICT, Development, and Poverty Reduction: Five Emerging Stories. *Information Technologies & International Development*, 6(SE), 11–17.

SSG Advisors. (April 2016). *Business Models for the Last Billion: Market Approaches to Increasing Internet Connectivity,* https://mstarproject.files.wordpress.com/2016/05/business-models-for-the-last-billion.pdf (last accessed 2 June 2019).

Team YS. (8 Aug 2019). Villgro's iPitch 2019: India's Marquee Social Impact Investors Come Together to Offer Rs 8 Crore Investment to Startups Looking for Seed to Pre Series A Funding. https://yourstory.com/2019/08/villgros-ipitch-2019-impact (last accessed 1 Sep 2019).

Teece, D. J. (2010). Business Models, Business Strategy and Innovation. *Long Range Planning*, 43(2–3), 172–194.

Thomas, A. (15 Jan 2019). *A New Lease of Life: How Bempu's Innovative Wristband Is Saving Thousands of Babies.* https://economictimes.indiatimes.com/small-biz/entrepreneurship/a-new-lease-of-life-how-bempus-innovative-wristband-is-saving-thousands-of-babies/articleshow/67535827.cms?from=mdr (last accessed 25 Oct 2019).

Thomas, A. (27 Sep 2018). How Rang De Is Using Crowdsourcing to Make Micro Loans Cheaper? https://economictimes.indiatimes.com/small-biz/money/how-rang-de-is-using-crowdsourcing-to-make-micro-loans-cheaper/articleshow/58509858.cms?from=mdr (last accessed 14 Sep 2019).

Tiwari, A. (8 Jun 2018). *Meet the Unsung Heroes of Waste Management – Rag-Picker Women.* https://yourstory.com/2018/06/rag-picker-women-unsung-heroes (last accessed 29 Sep 2019).

Tracey, P., & Phillips, N. (2007). The Distinctive Challenge of Educating Social Entrepreneurs: A Postscript and Rejoinder to the Special Issue on Entrepreneurship Education. *Academy of Management Learning & Education*, 6(2), 264–271.

UNDESA. (2019). World Population Prospects 2019. United Nations Department of Economic and Social Affairs. https://population.un.org/wpp/ Publications/Files/WPP2019_Highlights.pdf (last accessed 25 Nov 2019).

UNDESA. (21 June 2017). World Population Projected to Reach 9.8 Billion in 2050, and 11.2 Billion in 2100. United Nations Department of Economic and Social Affairs. www.un.org/development/desa/en/news/population/world-population-prospects-2017.html (last accessed 1 Dec 2019).

UNDP & Deloitte (September 2016). *Uncharted Waters: Blending Value and Values for Social Impact through the SDGs*, www.businesscalltoaction.org/sites/default/ files/resources/Unchartered_Waters_Report_BCtA_UNDP_Deloitte_Web_0 .pdf (last accessed 2 June 2019).

UNEP (2018). *Digital Finance and Citizen Action: In Financing the Future of Climate-Smart Infrastructure*, www.oecd.org/env/cc/case-study-digital-finance-and-citizen-action.pdf (last accessed 2 June 2019).

UN-POP (2019). www.un.org/en/sections/issues-depth/population/ (last accessed 1 Dec 2019)

Villgro Janitri. (2019). *Janitri Innovations*. www.villgro.org/janitri-innova tions/ (last accessed 26 Oct 2019).

Villgro Website. (2019). www.villgro.org/ (last accessed 1 Sep 2019).

VIR. (2018). Villgro Innovations Foundation Impact Report 2018. www.vill gro.org/wp-content/uploads/2019/05/Villgro_Impact-Report_Digital.pdf (last accessed 1 Sep 2019).

Viswanathan, M., & Sridharan, S. (2012). Product Development for the BoP: Insights on Concept and Prototype Development from University-Based Student Projects in India. *Journal of Product Innovation Management*, 29 (1), 52–69.

Viswanathan, M., Seth, A., Gau, R., & Chaturvedi, A. (2007). *Doing Well by Doing Good: Pursuing Commercial Success by Internalizing Social Good in Subsistence Markets*. Best Paper Proceedings of the Annual Meeting of the Academy of Management, Philadelphia, USA.

Viswanathan, M., Sridharan, S., & Ritchie, R. (2008). Marketing in Subsistence Marketplaces. In C. Wankel (Ed.), *Alleviating Poverty through Business Strategy*, 209–232. New York: Palgrave Macmillan.

Watson, B. (30 May 2014). *Serving the Base of the Pyramid: Five Tips from Emerging-Market Experts*. The Guardian. www.theguardian.com/sustain

able-business/2014/may/30/serving-the-base-of-the-pyramid-five-tips-from-emerging-market-experts#comment-36414158 (last accessed 16 June 2019).

WHO-IMR. (2019). Infant mortality. *World Health Organization.* www.who .int/gho/child_health/mortality/neonatal_infant_text/en/ (last accessed 26 Nov 2019).

WHO-MMR. (19 Sep 2019). Maternal mortality. *World Health Organization.* www.who.int/news-room/fact-sheets/detail/maternal-mortality (last accessed 26 Nov 2019).

WNR. (2016). *Sanitation Entrepreneur Mayank Midha in Talk with TWN. Water Network Research.* https://thewaternetwork.com/article-FfV/sanitation-entre preneur-mayank-midha-in-talk-with-twn–DRckzzgs5zpeeqgLQiILQ (last accessed 19 Oct 2019).

Woolcock, M., & Narayan, D. (2000). Social Capital: Implications for Development Theory, Research, and Policy. *World Bank Research Observer*, 15(2), 225–249

World Bank. (2 Oct 2019). Poverty. www.worldbank.org/en/topic/poverty/over view (last accessed 25 Nov 2019)

Yin, R. K. (2009). *Case Study Research: Design and Methods* (4th ed.). California: Sage Publications Inc.

YS. (12 Nov 2018). *Impactful Products That Indian IoT Startups Are Building as Part of the 3rd edition of the Qualcomm Design in India Challenge.* https:// yourstory.com/2018/11/indian-iot-startups-building-3rd-edition-qualcomm (last accessed 26 Oct 2019).

Yunus, M. (2010). *Building Social Business: The New Kind of Capitalism That Serves Humanity's Most Pressing Needs.* New York: Public Affairs.

Yunus, M., Moingeon, B., & Lehmann-Ortega, L. (2010). Building Social Business Models: Lessons from the Grameen Experience. *Long Range Planning*, 43, 308–325.

Cambridge Elements ≡

Economics of Emerging Markets

Bruno S. Sergi
Harvard University

Editor Bruno S. Sergi is an Instructor at Harvard University, an Associate of the Harvard University Davis Center for Russian and Eurasian Studies and Harvard Ukrainian Research Institute. He is the Academic Series Editor of the Cambridge *Elements in the Economics of Emerging Markets* (Cambridge University Press), a co-editor of the *Lab for Entrepreneurship and Development* book series, and associate editor of *The American Economist*. Concurrently, he teaches International Economics at the University of Messina, Scientific Director of the Lab for Entrepreneurship and Development (LEAD), and a co-founder and Scientific Director of the International Center for Emerging Markets Research at RUDN University in Moscow. He has published over 150 articles in professional journals and twenty-one books as author, co-author, editor, and co-editor.

About the Series
The aim of this Elements series is to deliver state-of-the-art, comprehensive coverage of the knowledge developed to date, including the dynamics and prospects of these economies, focusing on emerging markets' economics, finance, banking, technology advances, trade, demographic challenges, and their economic relations with the rest of the world, as well as the causal factors and limits of economic policy in these markets.

Cambridge Elements $\equiv$

Economics of Emerging Markets

Elements in the Series

Towards a Theory of "Smart" Social Infrastructures at Base of the Pyramid: A Study of India
Sandeep Goyal and Bruno S. Sergi

A full series listing is available at: www.cambridge.org/EEM

Printed in the United States
By Bookmasters